T0328642

Cambridge Elements

Elements in Historical Theory and Practice
edited by
Daniel Woolf
Queen's University, Ontario

A HISTORY OF POLITICAL SCIENCE

Mark Bevir
University of California, Berkeley

Shaftesbury Road, Cambridge CB2 8EA, United Kingdom

One Liberty Plaza, 20th Floor, New York, NY 10006, USA

477 Williamstown Road, Port Melbourne, VIC 3207, Australia

314–321, 3rd Floor, Plot 3, Splendor Forum, Jasola District Centre,
New Delhi – 110025, India

103 Penang Road, #05–06/07, Visioncrest Commercial, Singapore 238467

Cambridge University Press is part of Cambridge University Press & Assessment,
a department of the University of Cambridge.

We share the University's mission to contribute to society through the pursuit of
education, learning and research at the highest international levels of excellence.

www.cambridge.org
Information on this title: www.cambridge.org/9781009044295

DOI: 10.1017/9781009043458

First published 2022

A catalogue record for this publication is available from the British Library.

ISBN 978-1-009-04429-5 Paperback
ISSN 2634-8616 (online)
ISSN 2634-8608 (print)

A History of Political Science

Elements in Historical Theory and Practice

DOI: 10.1017/9781009043458
First published online: August 2022

Mark Bevir
University of California, Berkeley
Author for correspondence: Mark Bevir, mbevir@berkeley.edu

Abstract: This Element denaturalizes political science, stressing the contestability and contingency of ideas, traditions, subfields, and even the discipline itself. The history of political science is less one of scholars testing and improving theories by reference to data than of their appropriating and transforming ideas, often obscuring or obliterating former meanings, to serve new purposes in shifting political contexts. Political science arose in the late nineteenth century as part of a wider modernism that replaced earlier developmental narratives with more formal explanations. It changed as some scholars yoked together behavioural topics, quantitative techniques, and positivist theory, and as other scholars rejected their doing so. Subfields such as international relations remained semi-detached and focussed on policy as much as theory. Furthermore, the shifting fashions within political science – modernism, behaviouralism, realism, neoliberalism, the new institutionalism – have informed the policies by which governments have tried to tame contingency and govern people.

Keywords: political science, international relations, behaviouralism, political institutionalism, neoliberalism

ISBNs: 9781009044295 (PB), 9781009043458 (OC)
ISSNs: 2634-8616 (online), 2634-8608 (print)

Contents

1 Introduction

Numerous historians write about the ways in which states and societies have represented themselves. Many historians are acutely aware of the role that these representations have played in constructing and legitimating ways of life and public policies. Indeed, their studies often have a sceptical cast. They suggest that these representations, and so any policies based on them, are simplistic, parochial, and otherwise inadequate. Even if the representations initially appeared to be neutral or scientific accounts of social and political practices, historians now emphasize their partiality, contingency, and contestability.

In this Element, I treat political science as a series of such representations. I adopt a sceptical historicizing stance towards the accounts that political scientists have given of politics. In doing so, I challenge the ways in which many political scientists think about their discipline, its role in society, and its relation to history. Political scientists often think that they are, albeit slowly and collectively, advancing an empirical science. In contrast, I will argue that they generally rely on contingent and questionable theoretical assumptions. Political scientists often think that they are giving us knowledge of an external world. In contrast, I will emphasize the extent to which their ideas help to make the world. Political scientists often think that they incorporate history as data and as context. In contrast, I will suggest that they have yet to come to terms with history as explanation and as critique.

These contrasts arise because I rely on a historicism that undercuts the modernism that dominates political science. Modernism prompts political scientists to adopt formal and stylized representations of the world.[1] Historicism prompts me to offer sceptical narratives about these representations. Modernism and historicism themselves can be historicized. This Element is, indeed, an attempt to do just that. Its main narrative is straightforward. In the nineteenth century, human scientists generally made sense of the social and political world in ways that drew on a developmental historicism. They located political institutions in the history of the relevant state, and they saw that history as broadly rational and progressive. Today's social sciences, including political science, arose as this developmental historicism gave way to new modernist forms of understanding. Political scientists began to explain behaviour and institutions mainly by locating them within stylized systems or models and often with the aid of formal correlations. This modernist political science

---

[1] W. Everdell, *The First Moderns* (Chicago: University of Chicago Press, 1997); H. Heyck, *The Age of System: The Rise and Fracture of High Modern Social Science* (Baltimore: Johns Hopkins University Press, 2015); and D. Ross (ed.), *Modernist Impulses in the Human Sciences, 1870– 1930* (Baltimore: Johns Hopkins University Press, 1994).

inspired many of the policies and institutions that govern us today. Nonetheless, although modernist social science is widespread, there are alternatives. In particular, historicists have revised some of their assumptions. Few historicists today believe that history is rational and progressive. They offer sceptical narratives, emphasizing contingency and contestability.

Properly to historicize political science is, therefore, to challenge it. Much political science relies on modernist explanations. It offers synchronic explanations that refer to laws, correlations, mechanisms, and formal patterns. In contrast, historicist explanations are diachronic narratives. Although in the nineteenth century developmental assumptions restrained the centrifugal force of these narratives, the scepticism of today's more radical historicism serves precisely to undercut stylized and formal representations.

We should distinguish here between history and the kind of radical historicism to which I am appealing. Some approaches to history, and to the history of political science, do not have a critical impact. It is perhaps unsurprising that these approaches to history are the most common ones within political science itself. All political scientists would accept that history provides data: even rational choice theorists apply their formal models to the past. Some political scientists – including the self-described historical institutionalists – also appeal to history to fix the context in which their formal explanations apply. In their view, the past has created a set of institutions, but we can now explain the operation and development of these institutions using standard modernist techniques.

Political scientists typically think about the history of their discipline in ways that are historical without being properly historicist. Their internal histories are disciplinary histories written by political scientists for political scientists.[2] Internal histories generally treat political science as if it were a natural, or at least rational, field defined by a clear and distinct empirical domain. These histories implicitly or explicitly define political science by reference to the domain of politics and the shared intellectual agenda of making this domain the object of a cumulative science. Sometimes they suggest that this agenda and domain are perennial facts of human life, tracing political science back to

---

[2] M. Baer, M. Jewell, and L. Sigelman (eds.), *Political Science in America: Oral Histories of a Discipline* (Lexington: University Press of Kentucky 1991); D. Easton, J. Gunnell, and L. Graziano, *The Development of Political Science: A Comparative Survey* (New York: Routledge, 1991); J. Hayward, B. Barry, and A. Brown (eds.), *The British Study of Politics in the Twentieth Century* (Oxford:Oxford University Press, 1999). For a historical survey of disciplinary histories, see R. Adcock, 'A Disciplinary History of Disciplinary Histories: The Case of Political Science' in R. Backhouse and P. Fontaine, *A Historiography of the Modern Social Sciences* (Cambridge: Cambridge University Press, 2014), pp. 211–36.

classical Athens.[3] Sometimes they suggest that the agenda and domain arose out of the triumph of reason over theology, tracing political science back to the Scottish Enlightenment.[4] Sometimes they focus on the creation of an autonomous discipline, free from the clutches of history, law, and philosophy.[5] Then, once these internal histories have described the alleged origins of political science, they proceed to chart the progress it has made in its subsequent development. This progress might just consist in the growing professionalization, sophistication, and diversity with which political scientists discuss questions, or it might also consist of substantive contributions to better or even true knowledge of political phenomena and their causes.

Clearly, these internal histories are profoundly flawed. They suggest that we can divide intellectual history into the disciplines that we find in universities today, thereby underplaying the extent to which ideas from one discipline impact another. They suggest that scholars in a discipline respond primarily to its questions and debates, thereby underplaying the role of events in creating new agendas. They even suggest that the history of a discipline is a teleological process leading inexorably to the current status quo.

These flaws arise precisely because internal histories assume political science has a shared agenda based on a shared empirical domain. A more radical historicism challenges this assumption. Radical historicism makes historians wary of postulating a given empirical domain or a shared intellectual agenda as the defining feature of any putative discipline. It turns the constitution of a discipline from an assumption or a fulfilment into a problem. 'Disciplines are unstable compounds', as Stefan Collini once wrote, for 'what is called a "discipline" is in fact a complex set of practices, whose unity, such as it is, is given as much by historical accident and institutional convenience as by a coherent intellectual rationale'.[6] The creation of an apparently given empirical domain and shared intellectual agenda appears here as the contingent victory of particular intellectual traditions, where these traditions legitimate themselves precisely by telling the history of the discipline as if their own assumptions were unproblematic.

---

[3] G. Almond, 'Political Science: The History of the Discipline' in R. Goodin and H. Klingemann (eds.), *A New Handbook of Political Science* (Oxford: Oxford University Press, 1995), pp. 50–96.

[4] J. Farr, 'Political Science and the Enlightenment of Enthusiasm', *American Political Science Review*, 82 (1988), 51–69.

[5] W. Riker, 'The Two-Party System and Duverger's Law: An Essay on the History of Political Science', *American Political Science Review*, 76 (1982), 753–66; Almond, 'Political Science'.

[6] S. Collini, 'Postscript: Disciplines, Canons, and Publics: The History of "The History of Political Thought" in Comparative Perspective' in D. Castiglione and I. Hampsher-Monk (eds.), *The History of Political Thought in National Context* (Cambridge: Cambridge University Press, 2009), p. 298.

Although other historians have written excellent studies of ancient Greek ideas about politics, radical historicism denaturalizes the discipline in a way that points to a very different starting point for this history. People have long thought and written about politics. The modern discipline of political science, nonetheless, has relatively recent origins. If we are specifically interested in political science as one of a set of institutionally differentiated disciplines that together make up contemporary academic social science, then it was born in America early in the twentieth century.[7]

This history will give due prominence to the dominant role of America both then and now. Equally, however, we should be wary of a simple narrative of Americanization.[8] That narrative needs tempering with recognition of, for example, the influence of Europe on America and the way in which different European and other traditions have modified ideas adopted from America. The history of political science is, like all intellectual history, one of transnational exchanges in which ideas get appropriated and transformed. In what follows, I illustrate these exchanges mainly by using the British case as a counterpoint to the American one. I do not want thereby to suggest that Britain played a particularly important role. On the contrary, German scholarship was more influential on early American political science. I merely use Britain to illustrate the varying importance of diverse transnational exchanges across different aspects of political science. New empirical topics arose from exchanges in which British figures played as great an initiating role as Americans. New quantitative techniques often developed in America before being adapted in Britain. The new theories that arose in America have generally had at most a muted impact on British political science.

Radical historicists often emphasize the appropriation and transformation of ideas. They do so because they are sceptical of the naturalness or stability of disciplines. Radical historicists treat disciplines and subfields as contingent, changing, and contested both within and across national traditions. Consequently, although I share the concern of some political scientists and disciplinary historians to understand the present in light of the past that produced it, I think about both past and present in a way that breaks up the discipline. Instead of appealing to an empirical domain and the spread of knowledge about it, I look at the way scholars make and remake subfields and

---

[7] R. Adcock, 'The Emergence of Political Science as a Discipline: History and the Study of Politics in America, 1875–1910', *History of Political Thought*, 24 (2003), 481–508; D. Ross, *The Origins of American Social Science* (Cambridge: Cambridge University Press, 1991), chaps 3 and 8.

[8] R. Goodin and H-D. Klingemann, 'Political Science: The Discipline' in R. Goodin and H-D. Klingemann (eds.), *A New Handbook of Political Science* (Oxford: Oxford University Press, 1998), pp. 1–49.

approaches by drawing on diverse traditions characterized by competing assumptions. I unpack the contingent origins of dominant approaches, recover alternatives that drop out of narratives focussed solely on America, and question the naturalizing histories by which political scientists legitimate their own approaches as contributing to scientific progress. I do not seek to invert the naturalizing narrative of intellectual progress into a despairing narrative of stagnation or decline. Rather, I aspire to interpret the history of political science in a way that bypasses the narrative options of progress, stagnation, or decline.

Here radical historicism's wariness towards grand narratives and overarching categories raises the question: what sort of aggregate concepts, if any, should we use when studying the past? Disciplinary histories risk privileging the category of a discipline as if its institutions – for example, the American Political Science Association (APSA) or membership in Departments of Political Science – are boundaries to the flow of ideas and even explain the ways in which ideas develop within such boundaries.[9] Radical historicism encourages us to disaggregate the institutions of a discipline and thereby to portray them as the contingent products of debates that often include ideas that come from other disciplines. It encourages us, therefore, to deploy traditions as our aggregate concepts. Although these traditions might parallel the institutions of a discipline, they also might parallel specific subfields or cut across subfields and disciplinary boundaries. Radical historicism also casts doubt on accounts of ideational change that concentrate on debates about topics or objects – for example, politics, states, or globalization – that allegedly arise outside of particular traditions and of which scholars acquire better and better knowledge. It encourages us, instead, to understand traditions as changing as and when their exponents respond to inter-subjective dilemmas that arise within the context of particular traditions.[10]

Although radical historicists rely on concepts such as tradition and dilemma, they do not intend these concepts to capture stable or uniquely privileged descriptions. Their concepts serve, rather, to pick out patterns for particular purposes. On the one hand, therefore, the history I tell of developmental historicism, modernism, neoliberalism, radical historicism, and the like is just one simplified pattern among many that historians might describe. I describe broad trends that admit of exceptions: cases of developmental historicism still appear today, modernism can be divided into more subgroupings than I use, and so on. On the other hand, although historians should be sceptical of grand

[9] S. Collini, "'Disciplinary History' and 'Intellectual History': Reflections on the Historiography of the Social Sciences in Britain and France', *Revue de Synthese*, 3 (1988), 387–99.

[10] M. Bevir, *The Logic of the History of Ideas* (Cambridge: Cambridge University Press, 1999), pp. 174–264.

narratives and concepts that purport to pick out a fixed empirical domain, their narratives must use aggregate concepts if they are to be more than chronicles of one damn thing after another. What matters is that our aggregate concepts are suitably contingent, historicist, and pragmatic. Think of my history as a series of snapshots of the dominant approaches to political science from the late nineteenth century until today. Each snapshot relies primarily on American and British examples. Each snapshot includes references to its own simplifications. The point of the whole is to denaturalize political science and its representations.

2 The Rise of Political Science

Disciplines are social constructions. We could divide knowledge in all kinds of ways: for example, we could treat the social sciences as one single discipline, or we could treat political science, international relations, and public administration as distinct disciplines. Of course, once a discipline arises, we can attempt to trace earlier attempts to understand the topics and objects studied in that discipline. Equally, however, disciplines often arise in part because the relevant topics and objects are conceived in a way that takes them outside of existing disciplines. We should be cautious, therefore, of histories that assume the topics or objects are stable. We should explore the historical processes that move the topics and objects away from older disciplines to become the basis of a new discipline.

In the case of political science, people have long thought about political topics in ways that make them part of other disciplines or other modes of inquiry. Plato and Aristotle wrote about the polis from within their conception of philosophy. Throughout the nineteenth century, scholars generally treated politics as a branch of philosophy, law, and especially history. Any given state appeared to be a product of its past, constituted by its laws, and subject to moral assessment. The discipline of political science arose primarily because scholars began to think about political objects, such as the state, outside of these modes of inquiry. Moral assessment gave way to the ideal of a neutral science. A focus on constitutions and laws gave way to a growing emphasis on informal institutions and behaviour. Historical analysis slowly lost ground to more formal explanations. This section will examine how and why political science became this distinctive field of inquiry.

Developmental Historicism

Even in the late nineteenth century, few human scientists defined history and politics as separate disciplines. On the contrary, scholars called themselves Professors of History and Political Science all across America, from William

Sloane at Princeton, through Jesse Macy at Iowa, on to Bernard Moses at the University of California, Berkeley. The Whig historian, E. A. Freeman famously remarked, 'history is past politics; politics is present history'.[11] Far from being separate from history, political science was its continuation into the present. Furthermore, the same methods and explanations were appropriate to both history and contemporary politics. Human scientists sought objective narratives based on the systematic, impartial, painstaking, and rigorous collection and sifting of facts. Although some more deductive approaches flourished in the early years of the nineteenth century, by its end scholars identified scientific method with inductive rigour.[12] William Stubbs wanted histories to consist of painstaking 'chronologies of minutiae'.[13] Human scientists often contrasted their scientific narratives with the more partisan expressions of party politics. James Bryce suggested that political science took its materials from the historical study of the past before then applying them to the present, and that this inductive study of history was an important counterweight to excesses of party.[14] A rigorous historical study of politics was to guide statesmen.

Although human scientists emphasized their rigorous inductive methods, they collected and sifted facts within a type of framework that I will call developmental historicism.[15] In Britain, developmental historicism owed much to the conjectural histories of the Scottish Enlightenment. Enlightenment thinkers forged a science of society that explored the development of sociability in relation to a 'stadial' Whig historiography, culminating in patterns of exchange that they described as analogous to the movement of the planets. Developmental historicism also owed much to an organic or romantic outlook that emphasized the ability of living beings to make and remake social life through their activity, which expressed purpose, thought, and imagination. The conjunction of Whig historiography and organicism inspired numerous attempts to study politics within an

---

[11] G. Bremner and J. Conlin (eds.), *Making History: Edward Augustus Freeman and Victorian Cultural Politics* (Oxford: Oxford University Press, 2015).

[12] On the triumph of a Whiggish inductive approach over a Benthamite deductive one, see S. Collini, D. Winch, and J. Burrow, *That Noble Science of Politics* (Cambridge: Cambridge University Press, 1983). On America, see Adcock, 'The Emergence of Political Science as a Discipline', 481–508.

[13] W. Stubbs to E. Freeman, '13 April 1858' in W. Stubbs, *The Letters of William Stubbs*, W. Hutton (ed.) (London: Constable, 1904), p. 42.

[14] J. Bryce, 'Presidential Address to the Fifth Annual Meeting of the American Political Science Association', *American Political Science Quarterly*, 3 (1909), 10–16; W. Lecky, *The Political Value of History* (London: E. Arnold, 1892).

[15] For an explicit statement of the importance of 'philosophy' in ordering historical facts, see J. Burgess, 'Political Science and History' in *Annual Report of the American Historical Association for the Year 1896* (Washington: Government Printing Office, 1897), pp. 201–20.

evolutionary narrative.[16] Developmental historicists used organic and evolutionary ideas to frame narratives of the unfolding of the principles of nationality and liberty along clear paths. We find such narratives most famously in the Whig constitutional histories of Freeman, J. R. Green, and Stubbs. However, these narratives of progress also attracted both sides in the philosophical dispute between idealists and positivists. Although positivists followed August Comte, J. S. Mill, and, at times, Leopold von Ranke in promoting rigorous scientific methods, they identified evolutionary theory as the pinnacle of science, so they adopted developmental historicism as the setting in which to situate their empirical findings.[17] Sidney Webb hoped to foster this evolutionary positivism when he founded the London School of Economics in 1895. Likewise, although idealists thought of the absolute as spiritual perfection, they increasingly used Hegelianism and social organicism in ways that made developmental historicism the setting in which the absolute unfolded.[18] The Bosanquets drew on this organicist idealism when they faced the Webbs in the great Edwardian debate about social policy.[19] Developmental historicism dominated the human sciences during the late nineteenth century precisely because it could bring together conjectural Whig histories, theories of evolution, and accounts of the unfolding of divine providence.

Developmental historicists told narratives of continuity. They believed in the gradual triumph of the principles of nationality and freedom. As a result, they understood history and politics as continuous with one another. On the one side, they understand politics by locating it within a historical narrative. On the other side, they understood history by locating it in relation to a larger whole, the content and meaning of which derived from contemporary notions of nationality and freedom.

Generally, developmental historicists approached the study of politics through national histories that told of gradual changes in ideas, institutions, and practices of freedom as these triumphed over those of tyranny. Even when

---

[16] J. Burrow, *Evolution and Society* (Cambridge: Cambridge University Press, 1966); J. Burrow, *A Liberal Descent: Victorian Historians and the English Past* (Cambridge: Cambridge University Press, 1981); and Collini, et. al., *Noble Science*, chaps. 6 and 7.

[17] M. Bevir, 'Sidney Webb: Utilitarianism, Positivism, and Social Democracy', *Journal of Modern History*, 74 (2002), 217–52; S. Collini, *Public Moralists: Political Thought and Intellectual Life in Britain 1850–1930* (Oxford: Oxford University Press, 1991); and D. Ross, 'On the Misunderstanding of Ranke and the Origins of the Historical Profession in America' in G. Iggers and J. Powell (eds.), *Leopold von Ranke and the Shaping of the Historical Discipline* (Syracuse: Syracuse University Press, 1990), pp. 154–69.

[18] S. den Otter, *British Idealism and Social Explanation* (Oxford: Clarendon Press, 1996).

[19] A. McBriar, *An Edwardian Mixed Doubles: The Bosanquets versus the Webbs* (Oxford: Oxford University Press, 1987).

developmental historicists pointed to threats to freedom, they still conceived of its triumph as ensured by an evolutionary process; progress was built into the order of things. Developmental historicists grounded their national histories on an appeal to principles that appeared in time either as foundational facts or as unfolding ideals. The most important principles were the nation state and democratic liberty. Indeed, they thought that these principles went together in that democratic liberty arose in organic communities that had reached their highest form in the nation state. Americans drew on German historicism to argue that, as John Burgess wrote, 'the national state is the consummation of political history'.[20] They typically identified the American state with a principle of freedom, as in Herbert Adams' account of how American democracy had developed out of Teutonic 'germs'.[21] British Whig historians suggested that the English nation had an unbroken continuity found principally in its democratic institutions.

The developmental historicists thought nation states were organic units defined by ethical, functional, and linguistic ties as well as a shared past. Adams argued that the institutions of the state constituted 'the all-uniting element of civil society and of the common life of men'.[22] Often developmental historicists conceived of national histories as the gradual realization of Teutonic principles. These Teutonic principles allegedly had emerged among the tribes and village communities of Northern Europe before going on to flower in Britain or America. The principles supposedly gave rise to representative institutions, constitutional liberty, local self-government, and common law.[23] Continental Europe, and especially France, appeared, in contrast, as the home of unrestricted democracy, centralized authority, and codified law. Generally, this contrast between Anglophone and continental states rested on a historical argument about the evolution of civilizations, not a biological argument about

---

[20] J. Burgess, *Reminiscences of an American Scholar* (New York: Columbia University Press, 1934), p. 247. On the idea of the state, see J. Farr, 'Political Science and the State' in J. Brown and D. van Keuren (eds.), *The Estate of Social Knowledge* (Baltimore: Johns Hopkins University Press, 1991), pp. 1–21. On German historicism, see J. Herbst, *The German Historical School in American Scholarship* (Ithaca: Cornell University Press, 1965).

[21] H. Adams, 'Special Methods of Historical Study', *Johns Hopkins University Studies in Historical and Political Science*, 1 (1884), 25–137.

[22] H. Adams, 'Is History Past Politics?', *Johns Hopkins University Studies in Historical and Political Science*, 3 (1895), 171.

[23] For British examples, see H. Maine, *Ancient Law* (New York: Dutton, 1917); H. Maine, *Village Communities in the East and West* (London: John Murray, 1871); and J. Bryce, *Modern Democracies*, 2 vols. (London: Macmillan, 1921), vol.2, pp. 7–8. For American ones, see H. Adams, 'The Germanic Origins of New England Towns', *John Hopkins University Studies in Historical and Political Science*, 2 (1892), 5–38; and J. Burgess, *Political Science and Comparative Constitutional Law*, 2 vols. (Boston: Ginn & Co., 1891).

racial characteristics.[24] Developmental historicists identified civilizations with shared cultural and moral habits and so common social and political institutions. They located different civilizations at various stages of a broadly common process of evolution. England and America were what they were because of a history that had inspired within them individualism and self-reliance, a passion for liberty, a willingness to pursue enterprise and trade, and a practical capacity in contrast to abstract reason. Certainly, J. S. Mill vehemently opposed efforts to attribute 'diversities of conduct and character to inherent natural differences', arguing that they arose instead from different contexts, some of which provided 'a lack of adequate inducements'.[25]

Developmental historicism inspired national histories that expressed racialist themes in terms of civilizations. A civilization embodied principles that provided a basis for continuity as well as for gradual change in response to new circumstances. In the British case, this national history emphasized that rule was in accord with precedent and convention, rather than a written constitution, and that these precedents and conventions protected civil liberty and local government. The constitutional settlement of 1689 represented the moment when it became clear that the monarch had to obtain the consent of Parliament to raise taxes or make laws. Local government meant that there was no place for a centralized and powerful bureaucracy or police. Ancient institutions, such as the monarchy and House of Lords, had adapted to rising democratic demands. This gradual evolution had produced a balanced constitution that allowed for popular participation and respected civil liberties even while it retained checks on excessive power and its miss-use. In the American case, the founding of the republic could appear as the continuation of a Teutonic past inherited from Britain or as the creation of a new utopia. Either way, the American people expressed themselves in the revolution and the Constitution, thereby giving legitimacy to the offices of state. Thereafter American history had exhibited the development of the spirit and institutions of this founding from the local to the centre – often with the Civil War appearing as the final act of unification – and from a limited republic to the more democratic eras of Jefferson and Jackson.[26] Burgess described the constitutions of England, France, Germany, and America

---

[24] On civilizational and racialist strands in developmental historicism, see, respectively, P. Mandler, '"Race" and "Nation" in Mid-Victorian Thought' in S. Collini, R. Whatmore, and B. Young (eds.), *History, Religion, and Culture: British Intellectual History 1750–1950* (Cambridge: Cambridge University Press, 2000), pp. 224–44; and J. Stapleton, 'Political Thought and National Identity, 1850–1950' in Collini, Whatmore, and Young (eds.), *History, Religion, and Culture*, pp. 245–69.

[25] J. S. Mill, 'Principles of Political Economy' in *The Collected Works of John Stuart Mill* (Toronto: University of Toronto Press, 1963–91), Vol. 2, p. 319.

[26] G. Bancroft, *A History of the United States from the Discovery of the American Continent to the Present Time*, 8 vols. (Boston: Little, Brown and Co., 1860–74).

in a manner that purported to show that America had reached the highest stage of development in the evolution of liberty and democracy.[27]

I have described the broad content of the national histories through which nineteenth-century scholars approached the study of politics. The key point is that politics was not a separate field of study but rather an extension of these histories into the present. Developmental historicists made sense of politics and the state by means of narratives of continuity and progress. They conceived of these narratives as scientific in large part because they identified science with rigorous inductive studies theorized in comparative and evolutionary terms.[28] Professors of politics rarely thought of the field as a separate discipline. On the contrary, they thought of their subject matter as the study of the historical unfolding of principles. Introductory texts to politics often explicitly discussed these principles and the comparative stages of their historical development.[29] Political scientists used the narratives and techniques of developmental historicism to describe and explain political practices, to edify the public, and to guide policymakers. Generally, they saw themselves as historians as well as social scientists. In America, William Dunning helped to create the political science curriculum at Columbia University, and he was, at the time of his death, president-elect of the APSA. He was also a founding member of the American Historical Association who served as its president, and he was one of the best-known historians of the reconstruction era of his time. His works on political science deployed an inductive historical method to trace the unfolding of political ideas and their expression in national institutions. In Britain, when John Seeley introduced the inductive study of politics at Cambridge University, it was as part of the History Tripos. The study of politics at Oxford was also part of the History School until the 1920s and the creation of Modern Greats – philosophy, politics, and economics.

Modernist Empiricism

A separate discipline of political science arose only when developmental historicism lost its hold on the scholarly imagination. The decline of developmental historicism mirrors the crisis of historicism among German intellectuals.[30] German scholars worried that historicism was self-defeating and unable to support viable concepts of truth or ethics. More generally, the

---

[27] Burgess, *Political Science*.

[28] R. Adcock, *Liberalism and the Emergence of American Political Science: A Transatlantic Tale* (Oxford: Oxford University Press, 2014).

[29] See, for example, J. Seeley, *Introduction to Political Science* (London: Macmillan, 1896).

[30] H. Paul, 'A Collapse of Trust: Reconceptualizing the Crisis of Historicism', *Journal of the Philosophy of History*, 2 (2008), 63–82.

decline of developmental historicism overlaps with the rise of new modernist ideas in the late nineteenth century. Modernists in the sciences as well as the arts began to evoke discrete units, submerged desires, and experiments, rather than continuity, rationality, and progress. Arguably, however, modernism took off in large part because people could not reconcile developmental historicism with their experience of the First World War. The senselessness of the War destroyed people's faith in continuity, progress, and reason. In America and Britain, moreover, the Teutonic principle became associated with Germanic absolutism.

The First World War undermined the faith in progress and reason that informed developmental historicism. Although images and ideals of progress still appeared after the War, progress was increasingly seen as a contingent victory of human activity rather than an inevitable feature of history.[31] Some scholars suggested that future progress would depend on the creation of new sciences that could resolve the distinctive social problems of the modern world. The First World War strengthened calls for new social sciences even as it weakened the old developmental historicism.

It was in this context that many of the social sciences, including political science, arose as distinct disciplines. These new social sciences typically based themselves on an epistemology that I will call modernist empiricism. Modernist empiricism was atomistic and analytic. It broke up the continuities and gradual change of developmental narratives by dividing the world into discrete and discontinuous units. It then sought to make sense of these units by means of impersonal mathematical rules or formal analytic schemas. It used ahistorical calculations and typologies to define its narratives, or even to replace narrative forms of analysis and explanation. Certainly, modernist empiricists introduced new analytic frameworks for comparison. As early as 1921, Herman Finer added to his study of comparative government an analytic index of topics designed to enable readers to compare similar institutions across states.[32] Before long, Finer, and others such as Carl Friedrich, started to present their studies in analytic rather than historical terms. Their books approached comparative politics through a series of general cross-national categories, rather than in the context of a historical narrative of particular states.[33]

---

[31] J. Kloppenberg, *Uncertain Victory: Social Democracy and Progressivism in European and American Thought, 1870–1920* (New York: Oxford University Press, 1986); and D. Rodgers, *Atlantic Crossings: Progressive Politics in a Social Age* (Cambridge, MA: Harvard University Press, 1998).

[32] H. Finer, *Foreign Governments at Work: An Introductory Study* (New York: Oxford University Press, 1921).

[33] H. Finer, *Theory and Practice of Modern Government* (Westport, CT: Greenwood Press, 1970); and C. Friedrich, *Constitutional Government and Politics* (New York: Harper, 1937).

The First World War also challenged the principle of the nation state conceived as an expression of an organic unity, which, when expressed in popular sovereignty, was the basis of liberty. Even if political scientists still viewed the state positively as the expression of a general will or a common good, they typically did so in relation to a society that was itself legitimately pluralistic. Ernest Barker and A. D. Lindsay adapted the idealist tradition, for example, in ways that gave greater credence to pluralism. This changing concept of the state led political scientists to distinguish their discipline from law and ethics. Political scientists looked past what they now condemned as constitutional pieties to study what they now believed was the real back and forth of contemporary politics.[34] Some political scientists argued that social conditions had changed so dramatically that old constitutional norms were no longer fit for purpose. They wanted to study these new social conditions and behavioural patterns and perhaps to propose new principles and institutions fit for the twentieth century.[35] These proposals were, of course, to derive from the findings of their new empirical science of politics at least as much as from legal and moral principles. Indeed, the very concept of the state sometimes gave way to that of government. Government lacked the old associations with law, reason, and progress. It was a more neutral term, referring either to the aggregation of diverse interests and attitudes in a society or to the institutions that articulated, managed, and responded to these interests and attitudes.

Modernist empiricists brought atomistic and analytic modes of inquiry to bear on the study of government. They created a political science that focussed on issues of psychology and process at least as much as history, law, and philosophy. For a start, whereas developmental historicists had conceived of action as conduct infused with reason and morals, modernist empiricists thought of it as behaviour to be examined either independently of any assumptions about mind or else in terms of theories about hidden depths of the mind that often overwhelmed reason and morals. Even when developmental historicists such as Bryce suggested that political science concerned mental habits, they situated these mental habits in the context of historical narratives about organic communities whose evolution realized principles of nationality and liberty. In contrast, modernist empiricists such as Charles Merriam and Graham Wallas used surveys and statistics, often informed by an analytic psychology, to reveal atomistic attitudes and opinions.

In addition, whereas developmental historicists had thought about politics in terms of moral narratives and constitutional principles, modernist empiricists

---

[34] G. Wallas, *Human Nature in Politics* (London: Archibald Constable, 1908).

[35] C. Beard, *An Economic Interpretation of the Constitution* (New York: Macmillan, 1961); and G. Wallas, *The Great Society* (London: Macmillan, 1914).

did so in terms of interests, processes, and functions. Modernist empiricists drew on a diffuse functionalism developed in the other emerging social sciences, particularly sociology and anthropology. Of course, we can read aspects of functionalist reasoning back into nineteenth-century theorists such as Herbert Spencer. However, it was only in the early twentieth century that Bronislaw Malinowski, A. R. Radcliffe Brown, and others defined functional explanations as scientific in contrast to historical ones.[36] The functionalists attempted to explain social facts by reference to the contributions they made to the social order as a whole. Sometimes they explored the relationships between elements of the social whole in a way that may seem contrary to the atomization that characterized modernist empiricism. However, the functionalists generally conceived of the social whole as an abstract, or even universal, framework that made possible comparison and classification of atomized units across diverse societies. Functionalism thus overlapped with a systems approach to organizations in a way that promised to provide a transhistorical context for atomistic and analytic studies of behaviour and processes.

Obviously, we should not draw too sharp a rupture between modernist empiricism and developmental historicism. On the one side, Wallas had notoriously little immediate impact on British political science, while Merriam's supporters spent much of the 1930s lamenting the limited use of quantitative methods in American political science. On the other side, Whig narratives still dropped off the pens of Bryce and younger scholars such as Barker, while Charles Beard's historical studies of American politics remained the bestselling political science texts of the time and the standard textbooks in many universities. When political scientists remained committed to older narratives, however, they often sounded nostalgic. Novelists and poets, such as E. M. Forster and John Betjeman, just as much as political scientists such as Barker, wrote in ways that suggested the world to which they referred was a thing of the past.[37] The nineteenth century's expansive confidence in continuity, reason, and progress was no more.

Modernist empiricists introduced analytic and atomistic modes of inquiry, and new focuses on behaviour and processes. In Britain, Wallas stands out as a particularly forceful advocate of the new political science. He denounced older approaches to politics for being out of touch with political reality.

---

[36] A. Radcliffe-Brown, 'The Mother's Brother in South Africa', *South African Journal of Science*, 21 (1924), 542–55.

[37] S. Pederson and P. Mandler (eds.), *After the Victorians: Private Conscience and Public Duty in Modern Britain* (London: Routledge, 1994); and J. Stapleton, *Englishness and the Study of Politics: The Social and Political Thought of Ernest Barker* (Cambridge: Cambridge University Press, 1994).

He championed a political science based on quantitative techniques and a scientific psychology of habit, emotion, and non-rational inference. Even if we forget about Wallas, modernist empiricism wrought a shift in the study of the British state. The rise of atomization and analysis transformed the Whig historiography of the developmental historicists into the Westminster model. In the nineteenth century, British scholars had understood the state in terms of a historical narrative. The new political scientists approached the British state as a set of institutions that they could analyse and classify in comparison with other states. In their view, Britain was a unitary state characterized by parliamentary sovereignty, cabinet government, party control of the executive, and a loyal opposition. Ironically, however, at the same time as the new political scientists relegated the Whig narrative to background for the Westminster model, so the new focuses on behaviour and process highlighted aspects of British politics that did not fit well with this model. Political scientists noted a decline in the independence of Members of Parliament, the influence of unelected officials, and the activities of pressure groups and the media. The history of British political science is, in many ways, one of successive attempts to locate new data and new concerns in relation to a Westminster model that is the legacy of the developmental historicism of the nineteenth century.

The impact of modernist empiricism was even greater in America, perhaps partly because history had less cultural authority there. Even before the First World War, A. Lawrence Lowell used his mathematical training to undertake a statistical study of party voting in Britain and America.[38] After the War, Merriam and Walter Lippmann, the latter being a student of Wallas, promoted both the use of quantitative techniques and the study of behaviour in terms taken from an analytic psychology.[39] They encouraged political scientists to begin to examine electoral behaviour through aggregate analyses of official census data and electoral statistics. The rise of survey research was perhaps an even more significant development in American political science. The sociologist Paul Lazarsfeld, who had trained as a mathematician, founded the Bureau of Applied Social Research, which generated much of its income by undertaking market research while also writing academic studies of the data thereby generated.[40] Likewise, the University of Michigan formed a Survey Research Center where an interdisciplinary group of scholars worked through the 1940s and 1950s on

---

[38] A. Lowell, *Public Opinion and Popular Government* (New York: Longmans, 1913).

[39] C. Merriam, 'The Present State of the Study of Politics' in *New Aspects of Politics* (Chicago: University of Chicago Press, 1970), p. 63; and W. Lippmann, *Public Opinion* (New York: Harcourt, Brace and Co., 1922).

[40] P. Lazarsfeld, B. Berelson, and H. Gaudet, *The People's Choice: How the Voter Makes Up His Mind in a Presidential Election* (New York: Duell, Sloan, and Pearce, 1944).

four programs addressing economic, political, and organizational behaviour as well as methodology. They surveyed public opinion to create new data with which to explore political behaviour.[41] All of this survey research precluded historical or comparative approaches if only because neither the past nor other countries could offer similar data.

Modernist empiricists did not entirely reject history. Rather, they gave history a different and smaller place in the study of politics and so debates about public policy. Political scientists used history more as a source of data than as grounds for explaining those data. Their explanations relied less on narrative and more on atomization, classification, statistical correlations, and even the identification of functions within a system. History continued to attract attention, especially among political theorists. However, political scientists increasingly shunned original historical research, relying instead on syntheses of existing scholarship to provide the background to their studies of the behaviour and processes of contemporary politics. Beard even defended history by arguing that it was a source of data. The more aggressive Merriam argued that history was a barrier to the rise of a proper science of politics.

The Institutions of Political Science

As political scientists created a discipline apart from history, law, and philosophy, so they began to create their own institutions. Arguably, the transatlantic flow of ideas continued mainly to be from Europe to America throughout the interwar years. When Americans championed behaviouralism and pluralism, they drew inspiration from British scholars such as Wallas and Harold Laski. The American discipline also received European immigrants.[42] Carl Friedrich, a student of Alfred Weber, joined Harvard's department of political science in the 1920s and helped to consolidate its pre-eminence. Soon after a number of émigrés from the Nazi regime, such as Leo Strauss, Hans Morgenthau, and Karl Deutsch, became powerful intellectual presences within American political science.

Even if the intellectual initiative remained with Europe, American scholars pioneered the institutions of political science as an autonomous discipline. American political scientists were growing in confidence and becoming more independent of the academic metropoles of Britain, France, and Germany. They blazed a new disciplinary path. In 1903, they founded the world's first national political science association, the APSA, which in 1906 created a journal, the *American Political Science Review*. APSA had rapid and noteworthy success in

---

[41] A. Campbell, W. Miller, and P. Converse, *The American Voter* (Chicago: University of Chicago Press, 1960).

[42] G. Lowenberg, 'The Influence of European Émigré Scholars on Comparative Politics, 1925-65', *American Political Science Review*, 100 (2006), 597–604.

attracting members. An initial growth spurt took it from a membership of 204 in 1904 to 1,462 just over a decade later in 1915, and membership subsequently doubled during the interwar decades to cross the 3,000 mark by the early 1940s.[43] The members of APSA took the lead in forging departments devoted to political science understood as a field apart from history, philosophy, law, sociology, and economics.

America's institutionally differentiated political science went from being an anomaly to an international model only in the years around 1950. In the aftermath of the Second World War, America enjoyed heightened prestige because of its military ascendance, its role in the new international organizations, and its aid to European reconstruction. It was in this context that the recently founded United Nations Economic Social and Cultural Organization (UNESCO) set out in the late 1940s to promote political science. UNESCO's initiative spurred the founding of the International Political Science Association in 1949, and national level associations in France in 1949, Britain in 1950, and West Germany in 1951. Just as APSA had founded a journal some half a century before, so now did these new national associations: the Association Française de Science Politique began *La Revue Française de Science Politique* in 1951, the British Political Studies Association began *Political Studies* in 1953, and the Deutsche Vereinigung Politische Wissenschaft began *Politische Vierteljahresschrift* in 1960.

It is important to stress that the creation of these institutions of political science was not obvious or inevitable. For a start, it was only as modernist empiricism replaced developmental historicism that political scientists conceived of their discipline as independent of philosophy, law, and especially history. In the 1870s and 1880s, a different generation of scholars founded America's first research universities at Johns Hopkins and Columbia, and they had not thought of political science as a free-standing field. In addition, even after modernist empiricists began to define political science as a discipline, they did not always rush to create new institutions. On the contrary, the existence of an autonomous discipline of political science was a North American anomaly for almost half a century. Although the Canadians formed a national political science association in 1913, scholars in other countries were in no rush to imitate the path of institutional differentiation pioneered in America.

3 Modernist Moments

Political science is not a natural discipline exploring a clearly distinct empirical domain. It is a construction of the interwar years, when modernist empiricists

---

[43] A. Somit and J. Tanenhaus, *The Development of Political Science: From Burgess to Behavioralism* (Boston: Allyn and Bacon, 1967).

rejected historicism, turned to formal explanations, and so separated the discipline and its objects of inquiry from history, law, and philosophy. It might be tempting to believe that political science then became a stable and unified discipline constituted by the theories that established it. This belief appears in those histories that identify the rise of political science with the behavioural revolution or, more polemically, with positivism. These histories suggest that, for better or worse, political scientists reject the humanities and seek a positive science: political science may be a triumph of science or it may be a mistaken attempt to treat humans as objects, but it is at least a coherent discipline.

Actually, political science is less a coherent intellectual enterprise arising out of one great epistemic shift than it is an accidental compound of several loosely related intellectual fashions. Modernist empiricism is not the same as positivism. Furthermore, the behavioural revolution was not a unified movement inspired by positivism: modernist empiricists had already introduced new topics and techniques, and the behaviouralists merely tried, largely without success, to bring these under the control of a positivist theory. American post-war political science was, therefore, a contingent amalgamation of diverse moments. These moments emphatically did not have to go together. Indeed, they often did not do so as they spread from America to Europe and elsewhere.

Modernist Topics

The years around 1950 brought not one but two turning points in the history of political science. At the same time as new political science associations appeared in Europe, the American discipline experienced a wave of self-criticism in the behavioural revolution. When we discuss behaviouralism, however, we should not take its revolutionary self-characterization for granted. We can understand the relationship of behaviouralism to earlier political science only after we have a fuller grasp on the modernism of the interwar years.[44]

The rise of modernist modes of explanation occurred alongside a shift in the topics of interest to political scientists. Although these trends reinforced one another, they had distinct roots, and they did not always go together. In the early twentieth century, developmental historicists were already looking past topics associated with institutional history, constitutional law, and the philosophical theory of the state. They too believed that these old agendas reflected a pre-democratic Europe and so were inadequate for the mass-based politics that had developed with the extension of the suffrage. Scholars argued that the study of

---

[44] R. Adcock, 'Interpreting Behavioralism' in R. Adcock, M. Bevir, and S. Stimson (eds.), *Modern Political Science: Anglo-American Exchanges since 1880* (Princeton: Princeton University Press, 2007), pp. 181–208.

modern democratic politics had to cover mass-based political parties and public opinion as well as formal institutions and laws. James Bryce's *The American Commonwealth* devoted hundreds of pages to accounts of how parties and public opinion actually worked.[45] Although Bryce was British, his seminal book had a dramatic influence on American scholars, including A. Lawrence Lowell, who later repaid the transatlantic debt with his *The Government of England*.[46] In addition to writing books on each other's countries, Bryce and Lowell also did pioneering comparative work on contemporary politics in continental Europe and the British-settler colonies.[47]

Other new topics began to draw attention from political scientists in the interwar years. Bryce and Lowell had introduced topics associated with mass-suffrage societies, but they still thought of democracy in terms of the sovereignty of a collective will. In the interwar years, a new pluralism challenged such concepts of democracy and the state. Once again, the changes involved transatlantic exchanges. Although American pluralism later developed a distinctive hue, its rise owed much to British scholars and especially Harold Laski, who spent several years lecturing at Harvard and Yale. Laski brought the term 'pluralism' and British debates about sovereignty into the American academy.[48] These early transatlantic discussions of pluralism generally had a normative dimension. They rethought democracy to make it not just a principle of popular sovereignty but also a fair way to balance competing interests and values in diverse societies. In America, this pluralism combined with the new topics associated with mass-based politics to inspire studies of pressure groups. A string of future presidents of the APSA, including Peter Odegard, Pendleton Herring, and E. E. Schattschneider, built their careers on such studies.[49]

By the outbreak of the Second World War, American political scientists were referring to all the new empirical research on parties, public opinion, and pressure groups collectively as the study of 'political behaviour'. The state of the discipline volume put together by the APSA in the 1940s went so far as to hold that 'political behaviour has largely replaced legal structures as the

---

[45] J. Bryce, *The American Commonwealth*, 3 vols. (London: Macmillan, 1888).

[46] A. Lowell, *The Government of England*, 2 vols. (New York: Macmillan, 1908).

[47] A. Lowell, *Governments and Parties in Continental Europe*, 2 vols. (Boston: Houghton, Mifflin, 1896); A. Lowell, *Public Opinion and Popular Government* (New York: Longmans, 1913), esp. chap XII–XIV, appendix A; Bryce, *Modern Democracies*.

[48] J. Gunnell, 'Making Democracy Safe for the World: Political Science between the Wars' in Adcock, Bevir, Stimson (eds.), *Modern Political Science*, pp. 137–57.

[49] P. Odegard, *Pressure Politics: The Story of the Anti-Saloon League* (New York: Columbia University Press, 1928); P. Herring, *Group Representation before Congress* (Baltimore: Johns Hopkins University Press, 1929); E. Schattschneider, *Politics, Pressures, and the Tariff* (New York: Prentice-Hall, 1935).

cardinal point of emphasis among political scientists'.[50] If this claim was an overstatement, it still shows that the study of political behaviour was prominent in American political science before the 'behavioural revolution' of the 1950s and 1960s.

Modernist Techniques

The modernists generally viewed their discipline as a science. Like their nineteenth-century predecessors, they equated science with the rigorous and impartial collection and sifting of facts. However, as they detached rigour from progressive narratives, so they tied it to atomization and quantification. Graham Wallas argued that quantitative methods were key to the study of the new empirical topics associated with a mass-based politics.[51] Charles Merriam carried Wallas' enthusiasm for quantitative techniques across the Atlantic to the University of Chicago. Under Merriam's leadership, the Chicago department surpassed the previously dominant Columbia department in both the number of doctoral students it produced and its prestige in the discipline.[52] Merriam trained and then hired other quantitative political scientists, including Harold Gosnell and Harold Lasswell. These latter political scientists then trained some of the leading figures of the behavioural movement, including V. O. Key Jr and Gabriel Almond. The Chicago School was, however, the exception not the norm in the interwar discipline. By the mid-1920s, Harvard had surpassed both Columbia and Chicago in prestige and in the number of doctorates it produced. At Harvard, Carl Friedrich led a widespread scepticism towards quantitative analyses.[53] Whereas new empirical topics were widespread, quantification was often considered a distraction that had had mercifully little impact.[54]

Quantification became more widespread in political science only after the Second World War. It then drew heavily on interdisciplinary work from the interwar social sciences.[55] Psychology and sociology had pioneered the use of an array of quantitative methods. Post-war political scientists relied on transfers from these disciplines. The exemplary studies that suggested that quantitative

---

[50] E. Griffith (ed.), *Research in Political Science* (Chapel Hill: University of North Carolina Press, 1948), p. 224.

[51] Wallas, *Human Nature in Politics*, chap 5.

[52] M. Heaney and J. Hansen, 'Building the Chicago School', *American Political Science Review*, 100 (2006), 589–96.

[53] C. Friedrich, 'Review of *Quantitative Methods in Politics*', *American Political Science Review*, 23 (1929), 1022–7.

[54] Griffith, *Research in Political Science*, p. 213.

[55] For an important emphasis on interdisciplinarity, see J. Isaac, *Working Knowledge: Making the Human Sciences from Parsons to Kuhn* (Cambridge, MA: Harvard University Press, 2012).

techniques could produce valuable results in political science came not only from Almond, Key, and other products of Chicago, but also from scholars trained and even employed in psychology and sociology, including, respectively, Philip Converse and S. M. Lipset.

Survey research is the paradigmatic example of quantification. Much of the early work was interdisciplinary. Paul Lazarsfeld trained as a mathematician before turning to sociology and founding the Bureau of Applied Social Research. Lazarsfeld led the group that wrote *The People's Choice*, a pioneering statistical analysis of voters in the elections of 1940 and 1944.[56] At the end of the 1940s, the Social Science Research Council founded a Committee on Political Behavior with Key as its chair and with the explicit goal of 'improvement in methods'.[57] Another interdisciplinary group of scholars established a Survey Research Center at the University of Michigan with the expressed goal of developing methodologies with which to study economic, political, and organizational behaviour. This Michigan group refined various techniques of sampling, interviewing, and data analysis for survey research before then running a small nationwide survey during the 1948 election. At that point, Key's Committee stepped in by securing money from the Carnegie Corporation for a full-scale survey during the 1952 election and using the Michigan centre to carry out the survey. When the Carnegie Corporation and the Rockefeller Foundation supported another national survey in 1956, the funding went directly to the Michigan Center. The data from these elections provided the basis for the classic study, *The American Voter*.[58]

Quantification had an enormous impact on American political science. Between 1950 and 1970, the percentage of articles in the *American Political Science Review* that relied on surveys went from 0 per cent to almost 50 per cent. Since this dramatic rise, survey research has continued to inform about a third of the journal's articles from the 1980s through until today. The figures are even more striking if we look at quantitative analysis more generally. Since the 1970s, about two-thirds of articles published in the journal have been quantitative studies.[59]

Modernist Theory

Modernists studied new topics using new techniques, but they did not thereby challenge older notions of theory. Although political scientists no longer

---

[56] Lazarsfeld et al., *The People's Choice*.
[57] SSRC Committee on Political Behavior, 'Committee Briefs: Political Behavior', *Social Science Research Council Items*, 4 (1950), 20.
[58] Campbell et al., *The American Voter*.
[59] L. Sigelman, 'The Coevolution of American Political Science and the *American Political Science Review*', *American Political Science Review*, 100 (2006), 463–78.

conceived of history as progressive and rational, they still understood 'theory' to be scholarship focussed on historical ideas and their impact on institutional development. Political theorists themselves spent more time studying, teaching, and writing about texts from earlier times than they did attempting to produce novel theories. Other political scientists generally held a low-key empiricist notion of science as fact gathering and objective reporting, and this view of science did not lead political scientists to question the standing of historical research. Political scientists certainly did not see political theory as an obstacle to a scientific discipline. On the contrary, they thought that political theory played a useful supplementary role; it provided historical accounts of both the concepts they used and the institutions they studied. In the interwar years, leading scholars often thus combined modernist studies of institutions and behaviour with historical studies of ideas. Ernest Barker in Britain and Friedrich in America wrote comparative institutional studies, histories of ideas, and translations of canonical texts.[60]

Nonetheless, when modernists explored new topics, they raised issues that would eventually raise questions about what theory should be. The studies of the new topics lacked clear ties to political theory. The study of pressure groups developed, for example, less as an illumination of a new pluralist theory of democracy than as a critical analysis of obstacles to the realization of democracy conceived in older terms as the expression of a collective will. By 1940, the gap between empirical work and theory was becoming a locus of anxiety within the American discipline. Benjamin Lippincott in particular charged his fellow political scientists with atheoretical empiricism.[61] When Lippincott reiterated this complaint in UNESCO's 1950 worldwide review of political science, he was far from being a lonely voice. Most American contributors echoed his concerns.[62]

Although American political scientists shared a growing dissatisfaction with the relation of theory to empirics, they offered a plethora of different solutions. They all wanted a 'creative thinker' to 'give meaning to the painstaking research that, while indispensable, is still not enough'; but they disagreed profoundly about what such creative thinking involved.[63] Some political

---

[60] E. Barker, *Political Thought in England from Herbert Spencer to Present Day* (New York: Holt, 1915); E. Barker, *The Development of Public Services in Europe, 1660–1930* (New York: Oxford University Press, 1944); Aristotle, *The Politics*, E. Barker (trans.) (Oxford: Clarendon Press, 1946); C. Friedrich, *Constitutional Government and Democracy* (Boston: Little, Brown, 1941); C. Friedrich, *The Age of the Baroque, 1610–1660* (New York: Harper, 1952); and I. Kant, *The Philosophy of Kant*, C. Friedrich (trans.) (New York: Modern Library, 1949).

[61] B. Lippincott, 'The Bias of American Political Science', *Journal of Politics*, 2 (1940), 125–39.

[62] UNESCO, *Contemporary Political Science: A Survey of Methods, Research and Teaching* (Paris: UNESCO, 1950).

[63] Griffith, *Research in Political Science*, p. 237.

scientists were content with the existing order. Others thought that political science remained both too historicist and too instrumentalist. Émigré scholars, such as Hans Morgenthau and Leo Strauss, argued against relying on science and technology. They drew inspiration from canonical texts in which they found more realistic and more ethical approaches. Yet others argued, on the contrary, that the discipline should detach itself from old styles of theorizing. They wanted the discipline to develop new theories more suited to the contemporary age.

Modernists in particular often called for new theories to make sense of the data they were creating by bringing new techniques to bear on new topics. When the Committee on Political Behavior announced that the 'development of theory' was one of its core concerns, it had in mind this type of theory.[64] Canonical texts generally had little to say about industrial societies, mass politics, organized pressure groups, and statistical analysis. Modernist empiricists wanted new theories to make sense of their findings and to highlight future areas of research. As Pendleton Herring said in his 1953 APSA presidential address, theory was necessary to provide 'a conceptual scheme for the analysis and ordering of empirical data on political behaviour'.[65] In this view, theory was to synthesize existing research and, ideally, to direct future research to questions that would promote further scientific advances.

Positivist Theory

When, in 1953, David Easton diagnosed political science with 'hyperfactualism', he was, therefore, reformulating an already familiar complaint.[66] Easton argued that political scientists were mistakenly wedded to 'a view of science as the objective collection and classification of facts and the relating of them into singular generalizations'.[67] This view of science had led them to accumulate data without taking control of it. Easton's concept of hyperfactualism suggested that political scientists were overwhelmed by quantitative and qualitative data largely because they lacked a theoretical framework with which to make sense of it all. He argued that a proper science would produce 'reliable, universal knowledge about social

---

[64] 'Committee Briefs: Political Behavior', 20.

[65] P. Herring, 'On the Study of Government', *American Political Science Review*, 47 (1953), 968.

[66] D. Easton, *The Political System: An Inquiry into the State of Political Science* (New York: Knopf, 1953).

[67] D. Easton, *Political System*, pp. 65–6. On historiographies of behaviouralism see J. Farr, 'Remembering the Revolution' in J. Farr, J. Dryzek, and S. Leonard (eds.), *Political Science in History: Research Programs and Political Traditions* (Cambridge: Cambridge University Press, 1995), pp. 198–224.

phenomena', and that 'the purpose of scientific rules of procedure is to make possible the discovery of highly generalized theory'.[68]

Although Easton echoed familiar diagnoses, his prescription was more clearly positivist. Easton and other behaviouralists adopted a positivist concept of a 'general theory' that used a clearly defined set of axioms to deduce generalizations that could be evaluated against empirical data. They envisaged a systematic political science that would advance through the cumulative interplay of theoretical innovation and empirical research. A general systems theory would give rise to predictions about political behaviour. Empirical political scientists would test these predictions in ways that would lead to changes in the theory. It is important to recognize that this positivism was not the naïve atheoretical enterprise its critics suggest. On the contrary, it was an attempt to build a new type of theory; it was an attempt to elucidate and direct empirical studies by means of a universal, deductive, predictive, and verifiable theory.

This positivism stood out from the earlier calls for new theories in political science. It involved a far more radical reimagining of what theory should and, more emphatically, should not be. Positivists often provided only sketchy accounts of criteria by which they proposed to judge the scientific merits of different theories. They were clear, however, that positive theories would bear little resemblance to older historical, legal, and philosophical ones, or to the reformist pragmatism that had been widespread in political science in the first half of the century. Their positivism separated the scientific merit of a theory from its normative role. Their theories did not aim to produce good social and policy outcomes. They aspired to be ethically neutral and empirically sound.

Positivists developed particularly ambitious agendas in the subfield of comparative politics. This subfield expanded dramatically in size, scope, prestige, and funding in the post-war years. America was engaged in the Cold War, competing for the allegiance of the new nations emerging from decolonization in Africa and Asia. In the interwar years, when Friedrich and Finer had created new analytic frameworks for comparative study, they had grounded their categories in the historical experiences of Europe and America. By 1954, when the Social Science Research Council set up a Committee on Comparative Politics, chaired by Almond, the developing world was becoming at least as important. The Committee brought together scholars who aspired to remake their subfield by forging a general positive theory that would cover all countries. More specifically, they hoped to combine functionalism and systems

---

[68] Easton, *Political System*, pp. 24–5.

theory to create a general theory pitched at the macro-societal level.[69] These scholars drew inspiration from Easton, the American sociologist Talcott Parsons, and British social anthropology. These influences led to a distinctive set of concepts. Comparative political scientists adopted Easton's 'political system', rather than Parsons' 'social system'.[70] Later, when they began to explore changes within political systems, their key term was 'political development', rather than the sociological 'modernization'.[71]

Positivism versus Modernism

By 1960, most of the social sciences were entangled with a positivist concept of science. Positivism undoubtedly appealed to social scientists in part because it legitimized their claims to expertise. Although economists played the largest role in directing the expansion of state activity after the Second World War, other social scientists could advance their claims to play a similar role by presenting their field as positivist during what was a time of optimism about technocratic reform. Indeed, because state funding for social science favoured scientism and policy relevance, social scientists were more likely to get employment, grants, and promotions if they presented themselves as being loosely positivist.

The rise of positivist social science led to a further denigration of history and narrative. Yet, positivism challenged modernism almost as much as it did developmental historicism. For a start, positivists typically defended a more demanding concept of science than that of inductive rigour. They exhorted political scientists critically to examine and improve their methods, and they associated such improvement almost exclusively with the new statistical techniques of data analysis. Although quantification is not a necessary companion of methodological sophistication, the positivists often seemed to think otherwise. More importantly, positivists defended a new concept of theory as both general and deductive. Consequently, they denigrated the inductive correlations and classifications of modernists as mere lower-level generalizations that needed incorporating in a universal theory such as systems theory or structural functionalism.[72] Although modernists had used functionalist explanations,

---

[69] G. Almond, 'A Functional Approach to Comparative Politics' in G. Almond and J. Coleman (eds.), *The Politics of the Developing Areas* (Princeton: Princeton University Press, 1960), pp. 3–64.

[70] Easton, *Political System*; M. Fortes and E. Evans-Pritchard, *African Political Systems* (London: Oxford University Press, 1940).

[71] G. Almond, 'A Developmental Approach to Political Systems', *World Politics*, 17 (1965), 183–214.

[72] Easton, *Political System*; and G. Almond, 'Functional Approach'.

positivists consciously crafted functionalist theories and concepts at a sufficiently abstract level to suggest that they had general applicability.

We should not be surprised, therefore, that several prominent modernists expressed grave doubts about positivist agendas. Leading figures of the elder generation voiced concerns about the universal and deductive nature of positivist theory. Friedrich responded to an early report from the Committee on Comparative Politics by arguing that comparative politics should focus on problems that were historically specific to certain states at certain points in time. He suggested that the subfield would lose contact with such problems if it pursued 'excessive abstraction'.[73] These concerns soon spread to some younger political scientists who had flirted with positivism. In the late 1950s, Samuel Beer, a Harvard scholar of British politics, had praised the 'structural-functional' theory of the 'political system' as the polestar guiding the way to a general comparative science.[74] By the early 1960s, he had changed his mind; he began to attack the 'dogma of universality' and the 'utopia of a universal theory'.[75]

Other political scientists also rejected positivist theory for the modernism that had dominated the interwar years. They pursued empirical studies and analytical comparisons, while expecting that generalizations and theory would be contextually limited in their reach. Although they rejected positivist theory, they often remained committed to modernist topics. Beer, for example, continued to write on British parties and pressure groups in a new age of mass politics and collectivism.[76] Some political scientists downplayed positivist theory while extolling not only behavioural topics but also quantification and statistical analysis. In his 1958 presidential address to APSA, Key, who had moved to Harvard in 1951, praised 'systematic analysis' while expressing doubts about general deductive theorizing. He argued that 'grand hypotheses' might offer beguiling 'psychic satisfactions', but they failed to come to terms with the 'incorrigibility' of political data. He urged political scientists to seek 'modest

---

[73] C. Friedrich, 'Comments on the Seminar Report', *American Political Science Review*, 47 (1953), 658–61.

[74] S. Beer, 'The Analysis of Political Systems' in S. Beer and A. Ulam (eds.), *Patterns of Government: The Major Political Systems of Europe* (New York: Random House, 1958), pp. 3–68.

[75] S. Beer, 'Causal Explanation and Imaginative Re-enactment', *History and Theory*, 3 (1963), 6–29; S. Beer, 'Political Science and History' in M. Richter (ed.), *Essays in Theory and History: An Approach to the Social Sciences* (Cambridge, MA: Harvard University Press, 1970), pp. 41–73.

[76] S. Beer, 'Pressure Groups and Parties in Britain', *American Political Science Review*, 50 (1956), 1–23; and S. Beer, *Modern British Politics: A Study of Parties and Pressure Groups* (London: Faber, 1963).

general propositions' and to remember that the 'verified general proposition of one era may not hold at a later time'.[77]

The Limits of Americanization

Once we disaggregate behaviouralism into new topics, techniques, and theories, we are better able to track its history. All too often, the history of political science or even the social sciences more generally appears to be one of the diffusion of, and resistance to, an American agenda. These histories are misleading. We have already seen that modernism, including behavioural topics, developed partly through transnational flows from Europe to America. We should not be surprised, therefore, that behavioural topics flourished in Europe as well as America. British scholars between the wars explored all the main behavioural topics apart from pressure groups. Research into British pressure groups arose only in the 1950s, some thirty years after it did in America. It is true that empirical work on behavioural topics was less extensive in Britain than in America, but that contrast reflected the size of the discipline in the two countries. In 1950, when the British Political Studies Association was founded, it had about 100 members, whereas APSA had over 4,000 members in the 1940s.

As quantification was a more clearly American trend, it made slow headway in Europe. But it is important to distinguish here between different quantitative techniques and the extent to which they already had a place in European social science. For example, British survey research long predated American behaviouralism. At the end of the nineteenth century, Charles Booth, Henry Mayhew, and Seebohm Rowntree conducted surveys of urban poverty.[78] One of Booth's assistants was Beatrice Webb, a leading Fabian socialist, and in the twentieth century, socialist and radical groups, including the New Fabian Research Bureau, conducted surveys into a vast array of social issues, inaugurating a style of activist research that prompted survey work among American progressives.[79] British political scientists were well prepared to extend survey work to voting behaviour, and they duly began the Nuffield election studies in 1945.[80] Nonetheless, the evolution of election studies in Britain shows a clear debt to American behaviouralism. Before long, David Butler came to dominate the Nuffield studies, and his approach owed much to his collaboration with

---

[77] V. Key, 'The State of the Discipline', *American Political Science Review*, 52 (1958), 961.

[78] D. Englander and R. O'Day (eds.), *Retrieved Riches: Social Investigation in Britain, 1880–1914* (Aldershot: Scolar Press, 1995).

[79] Rodgers, *Atlantic Crossings*; and Kloppenberg, *Uncertain Victory*.

[80] R. McCallum and A. Readman, *The British General Election of 1945* (London: Oxford University Press, 1947).

Donald Stokes, an American scholar from the University of Michigan.[81] If Butler adopted statistical analysis to assess the relative weight of various causal factors, large chunks of the Nuffield studies continued to be written in a kind of high table, insider style, with a suggestion of privileged information as the basis for informed accounts of the strategies and personalities involved in election campaigns. British political science confronted calls for a more extensive use of quantitative techniques only in the 1960s and 1970s, with the rise of Richard Rose, an American, at the University of Strathclyde, and Jean Blondel, a Frenchman, at the University of Essex. The use of surveys and statistical analysis then spread, as it had in America, from election studies to political culture, socialization, and other areas such as race.[82]

Finally, as positivist theory was an American creation, it had little impact in Europe. When quantitative scholars in Europe wrote about theory, they, like Key in America, made concessions to modernism. For example, although Blondel wrote that political science required quantification to distinguish it from journalism, he also suggested that politics was too messy to be studied scientifically, that general theories were too ambitious, and that political scientists should aim at mid-range theories and limited comparisons.[83]

Political science arose and developed in a wide range of transnational exchanges. Ideas were constantly overpowered, dominated, adjusted, and reinterpreted. Their former meanings and purposes were often obscured or obliterated. They were often yoked together in temporary and unstable relationships. Narratives that recount the rise of a coherent discipline or a dominant positivism domesticate the contingency and contests involved. For a start, American political science included various warring factions, inspired by different ideas. These factions often forgot the history of their own ideas even as they forged them anew in the heat of a different battle. In addition, these warring factions appropriated ideas from other disciplines, sometimes with only a tentative understanding of them. They grabbed any likely looking weapon from any source they could and then tried to integrate those weapons with their existing armoury. Finally, ideas flowed back and forth across the Atlantic and no doubt, if I were able to trace them, in and out of Africa, Asia, and South America. Transnational alliances and debts often arose – perhaps acknowledged, perhaps denied, perhaps falsely claimed – as ways of boosting weaponry or morale in a local conflict.

---

[81] D. Butler and D. Stokes, *Political Change in Britain: Forces Shaping Electoral Choice* (New York: St. Martin's Press, 1969).

[82] R. Rose, *Politics in England: An Interpretation* (London: Faber, 1965).

[83] J. Blondel, *Discipline of Politics* (London: Butterworth, 1981), p. 109.

4 Thinking Globally

The social sciences arose as modernists replaced historical narratives with formal comparisons and explanations. Just as this shift was contingent and contested, so were the resulting divisions among the social sciences. We have already seen how political scientists drew on interdisciplinary ideas to create modernist and positivist agendas. In addition, we should note that disciplines themselves were neither stable nor homogenous. Modernists could have divided the social world in all kinds of ways. It was neither necessary nor especially rational for them to privilege, for example, politics, sociology, economics, and anthropology. All of these disciplines contain subfields that could just as reasonably have been located in other disciplines or even created as independent disciplines.

Public administration is one illustration of the arbitrariness of disciplinary boundaries within the social sciences. In America, the study of public administration often takes place in separate professional schools. Departments of political science give it some coverage, but the graduate programs are more prominent. Furthermore, scholars of public administration are often in close contact with faculty in other professional programs, including business schools. Historically, the American study of public administration has often been part of a broader cluster of organizational and administrative sciences.[84] Its theoretical and empirical concerns owe as much to analogies between public and private organizations as to a distinctive concern with the state and politics. Professional business schools and especially policy schools arose much later in Europe. In Britain, the study of public administration took place alongside the study of local government in departments of politics. In parts of continental Europe, with their Roman law rather than common law tradition, public law was part of a general legal education, and the more behavioural field of public administration barely existed before the 1950s.

International relations provides another illustration of the historical construction and peculiarities of subfields within or outside political science.[85] This section uses the example of international relations to highlight two other general points. First, the general characteristics of modernism spread in very uneven and different forms across subfields. Although international relations was made

---

[84] H. Heyck, 'Administrative Science' in M. Bevir, (ed.), *Modernism and the Social Sciences: Anglo-American Exchanges, c. 1918–1980* (Cambridge: Cambridge University Press, 2007), pp. 155–81; H. Crowther-Heyck, *Herbert A. Simon: The Bounds of Reason in Modern America* (Baltimore: Johns Hopkins University Press, 2005); and W. Scott, *Chester I. Barnard and the Guardians of the Managerial State* (Lawrence: University Press of Kansas, 1992).

[85] For a comprehensive history including institutions, organizations, and journals, see J.-A. Pemberton, *The Story of International Relations*, 3 vols (London: Palgrave Macmillan, 2020).

by modernism, its topics, techniques, and theories all show the effects of thinking about states as actors on the global stage. Second, much of political science concerned itself with events and policies at least as much as with the broad scientific and theoretical agendas outlined in the previous section. Although international relations had debates between historicists, modernists, and positivists, its main arguments for much of the twentieth century pitted liberals against realists in America and liberals against Marxists in Europe.

Modernizing Internationalism

In the early twentieth century, political scientists broke with history, law, and philosophy because they believed that these older topics reflected a pre-democratic Europe rather than the mass-based politics that had developed following the extension of the suffrage. International relations scholars rarely echoed this concern. Their world was still one in which states pursued diplomacy, managed conflicts, and fought wars. Nonetheless, the experience of the First World War had an equally dramatic impact on the study of international relations. For much of the nineteenth century, liberal scholars and politicians typically believed that history was progressing towards some sort of perpetual peace. Many of them believed that the nation state was a noble expression of the human spirit, and as the peoples of the world formed self-governing states, so there would be few remaining sources of conflict. States would manage and resolve any remaining conflicts through the balance of power and international law. The First World War overturned this complacent liberalism. It suggested that nation states were aggressive; they pursued imperial expansion and so came into conflict with one another. It suggested that politicians and voters were all too ready to tread jingoistic paths to war.

Scholars of international relations shifted to different topics less because of a concern with the distinctive conditions of modern society than because of a renewed fear of wars. This fear meant that they too turned away from the state. Whereas they had thought of the state as the highest form of political development, they now often blamed it for wars. Goldsworthy Lowes Dickinson argued, in his seminal book, *The International Anarchy*, that 'whenever and wherever the anarchy of armed states exists, war does become inevitable'.[86] International relations scholars reacted to this vision in two overlapping but distinct ways. On the one hand, scholars rejected old idealist and ethical concepts of the state. They looked instead to concepts that caught the kind of competition and 'power politics' that states seemed to practice on the international stage. Some explored the nature, sources, and uses of power itself.

---

[86] G. Dickinson, *The International Anarchy, 1904–1914* (New York: The Century, 1926).

In so far as they understood power as a descriptive term, they began to offer a more 'realistic' account of politics. On the other hand, liberals continued to believe in the normative ideals of managing power and promoting peace. They thus treated this realism as a spur to develop policy agendas based on international law and international institutions.

In international relations, the dominant topics of the interwar years were less behavioural ones than those associated with the rise of realist analysis and liberal aspirations. These topics proved far less amenable to survey research than did, for example, voting behaviour and political culture. Quantification first appeared in international relations, therefore, as a stylized approach to data. International relations experts began to quantify the study of war. They classified and counted past events in an attempt to answer key questions about the causes of war and peace, victory and defeat, and so on. Quincy Wright pioneered such work in the interwar years when he worked at Chicago.[87] Later, in 1963, J. David Singer set up the Correlates of War Project at the University of Michigan.

The new topics in international relations largely transcended the theoretical controversies that occupied other subfields of political science. Modernists sometimes turned from history to atomization, formal classifications, functionalist tropes, and even correlations, as in Wright's study of war. Generally, however, modernists loosened the ties of international relations to history without binding it to either new techniques or new theories. Many of them continued to treat international relations as a practical craft at least as much as a theoretically driven science. International relations scholarship drew on a range of somewhat incompatible theories and agendas in order to steer national policy and promote international institutions. Much international relations scholarship was, therefore, a lightly revised version of the classical internationalism of the nineteenth century. Internationalists designed institutions to regulate the relations of states, advance peace, and forge a new world order.[88] Their scholarship sought to help enforce international law, arbitrate disputes, and regulate transnational trade by promoting both international institutions and liberal democratic reform within states.[89] After the First World War, this internationalism inspired both the League of Nations and the

---

[87] Q. Wright, *A Study of War* (Chicago: University of Chicago Press, 1942).

[88] E. Aksu (ed.), *Early Notions of Global Governance: Selected Eighteenth-Century Proposals for 'Perpetual Peace'* (Cardiff: University of Wales Press, 2008); A. Williams, *Failed Imagination? The Anglo-American New World Order from Wilson to Bush* (Manchester: Manchester University Press, 2007).

[89] F. Halliday, 'Three Concepts of Internationalism', *International Affairs*, 64 (1988), 187–98.

attempt to implant liberal democratic regimes in the new states of Central and Eastern Europe.

Some international relations scholars saw the rise of fascism and the outbreak of the Second World War less as challenges to their craft than as further evidence of its overwhelming importance. Liberal internationalists continued to focus on cooperative institutions, agencies, and laws.[90] Many of them acknowledged that the League of Nations had glaringly failed to provide a forum for the peaceful resolution of disputes, and they moved away from its reliance on conference diplomacy and on collective security based on unanimity. They turned instead to international organizations that gave privileged status to key states, as did the United Nations Security Council, or to special agencies with clearly defined functional roles.

When international relations scholars turned to modernist theories, such as functionalism, they were, therefore, reacting to policy agendas at least as much as scientific ones. The failure of the League of Nations encouraged them to explore federalism, functionalism, and planning theory. Some federalists argued that problems such as war and global inequality needed more dramatic actions than those proposed by classic internationalists. They called for the progressive creation of a world state by treaty. They feared a war between the super powers might result in a world state imposed by force.[91] They wanted instead to get agreement on a federal constitution for a world government. Functionalists drew inspiration from the practical experience and relative success of existing specialized agencies as well as sociological theorists such as Talcott Parsons. David Mitrany, the most prominent early functionalist, argued that peaceful relations between states could emerge from functional agencies addressing discrete transnational problems.[92] Peace would arise as agencies progressively reduced issues of conflict between states, turned political disputes into technical ones, and so bound states in ever-closer relations. Planning theory often overlapped with functionalism. Scholars blamed the 'planlessness of the liberal order' for the 'anarchy' of the first half of the twentieth century. They advocated those forms of planning that they thought would 'allow a maximum of freedom and self-determination'.[93] This planning would remove the

---

[90] For legalist institutionalism, see A. E. Zimmern, *The League of Nations and the Rule of Law, 1918–1935* (London: Macmillan, 1936). For functionalist institutionalism, see D. Mitrany, *The Functional Theory of Politics* (London: M. Robertson, 1975); and E. Haas, *Beyond the Nation-State: Functionalism and International Organization* (Stanford: Stanford University Press, 1964).

[91] W. Lloyd, 'The United Nations and World Federalism', *The Antioch Review*, 9 (1949), 16–28.

[92] D. Mitrany, *A Working Peace System* (London: Royal Institute for International Affairs, 1943).

[93] K. Mannheim, *Man and Society in an Age of Reconstruction: Studies in Modern Social Structure*, E. Shils (trans.) (London: Routledge & Kegan Paul, 1940), p. 7.

insecurity and irrationality of the constant turmoil of free markets, thereby resolving the competition and conflict they believed characterized classical liberalism.

Internationalism, federalism, functionalism, and planning all shaped the international order that arose after the Second World War. A reformed internationalism informed the United Nations. Federalism influenced the European Economic Community as well as post-colonial states with federal constitutions, such as Malaysia and Nigeria.[94] Functionalism, too, influenced the European Economic Community in addition to specialized agencies within or outside the United Nations: some seventy new agencies were formed between 1943 and 1970.[95] Planning theory influenced international, regional, state, and specialist actors, many of whom fused it with ideas emerging from the new field of development theory. It flourished in the global institutions set up at Bretton Woods and among the policy experts who helped create and staff those institutions.[96] These experts hoped to promote liberal internationalist goals by intervening in ways defined by new modernist forms of social science.[97]

Realists and Liberals

While liberal internationalists thus updated their policy agendas, other international relations scholars argued forcefully that the rise of fascism and the outbreak of the Second World War showed that these old policy agendas were bankrupt. Throughout political science, émigrés from Nazi Germany took aim at both nihilism and scientism. Generally, they thought that fascism required a staunch moral response and they feared that technocratic modernists lacked the backbone to provide that response. They recognized the brutality of political power, and they thought the best way to restrain it was by appealing to tried and tested forms of order such as natural right or the balance of power.

Hans Morgenthau and other 'classical realists' brought this sensibility to the study of international relations. Morgenthau was born into a Jewish family in Coburg, Germany, in 1904.[98] He studied law and politics in Berlin, Frankfurt,

---

[94] D. McKay, *Federalism and the European Union: A Political Economy Perspective* (Oxford: Oxford University Press, 1999); D. Rothermund, 'Constitution Making and Decolonization', *Diogenes*, 53 (2006), 9–17.

[95] C. Murphy, *International Organization and Industrial Change: Global Governance since 1850* (Cambridge: Blackwell, 1994), pp. 154–7.

[96] G. Ikenberry, 'The Political Origins of Bretton Woods' in M. Bordo, J. Barry and B. Eichengreen (eds.), *A Retrospective on the Bretton Woods System* (Chicago: University of Chicago Press, 1993), pp. 155–82.

[97] N. Gilman, *Mandarins of the Future: Modernization Theory in Cold War America* (Baltimore: Johns Hopkins University Press, 2003).

[98] C. Frei, *Hans J. Morgenthau: An Intellectual Biography* (Baton Rouge: Louisiana State University Press, 2001).

Munich, and Geneva. He fled Germany in 1937 and eventually made it over to the United States. Thereafter he taught at Brooklyn College, the University of Kansas City, the University of Chicago, City College of New York, and the New School for Social Research. Under the influence of Friedrich Nietzsche, Carl Schmitt, and Max Weber, he reacted against nineteenth- and twentieth-century versions of liberal progressivism. In doing so, he blurred the distinctions I have been making between developmental historicism, modernism, and positivism. In his view, they were all too optimistic and, specifically, too ready to believe in their visions of science and its ability to remake the world. He argued instead for a realist theory that emphasized self-interest and power.

Morgenthau defined his realism by six key principles. Politics is governed by laws based on facts about human nature. Politicians pursue their interests and more particularly power. The nature of interest and power varies across contexts. All moral goals have to be adapted to allow for this pursuit of power. Politicians should act prudently in the national interest rather than, say, identifying their goals with morality itself. And politics should not be reduced to ethics or law.[99] Although this realism includes all kinds of ambiguities and confusions, it offers a clear account of international relations. Politics is about power. International relations scholars should study the ways in which power operates. Politicians should pursue the national interest, recognizing that others will do likewise. Idealist visions and technocratic policies are more likely to lead to misunderstanding and even war than to do good since they neglect power. Peace arises from a stable and clearheaded balance among the interests of various states.

Clearly Morgenthau's realism was less a vision of a scientific discipline than an account of human nature and a policy agenda. One can imagine historicists, modernists, positivists, and others all debating its validity. Somewhat confusingly, however, Morgenthau pitched his account of politics and especially his policy agenda against the idea of a science of politics. He contrasted a realist belief in the universal laws of human nature and power politics with a positivist belief in a cumulative science based on sociological theories, testable hypotheses, and empirical rigour. He suggested that international relations scholars look at history to trace the concrete ways in which power operated. Similarly, he contrasted a realist belief in prudent policies adapted to changing configurations of power with a positivist belief in technocratic expertise. He suggested that international policymaking should be risk averse statecraft pursuing national interests and peace.

---

[99] H. Morgenthau, *Politics Among Nations: The Struggle for Power and Peace* (New York: Knopf, 1954). The first edition was published in 1948, but he only introduced the six principles in the second edition.

This classical realism dominated the American study of international relations through the 1950s and 1960s. Kenneth W. Thompson, Morgenthau's former student, became a powerful figure at the Rockefeller Foundation. In 1954, Morgenthau used Rockefeller funding to convene the American Committee on the Theory of International Politics. The Theory Conference fended off trends in the rest of the social sciences. Most participants shared the vision of international relations as a field defined by a distinctive domain – the pursuit of power by states – that was impermeable to scientific rationalism.[100] Morgenthau, and other classical realists, including W. T. R. Fox, George F. Kennan, Reinhold Niebuhr, Paul Nitze, and Arnold Wolfers, proved extremely influential both in the academy and as policy advisers.

International relations scholarship thus saw relatively little of the positivism associated with functionalism and systems theory. There were notable exceptions, of course: Morton Kaplan's *System and Process in International Politics*, Karl Deutsch's work on *The Nerves of Government*, and in Britain John Burton's idiosyncratic *International Relations: A General Theory*.[101] Generally, however, international relations theory appealed to stylized pictures of human nature to delineate a world of power politics. Arguably, the main differences were those within classical realism between the Christian or Augustinian realists who stressed the inherent sinfulness and cupidity of human nature and the Hobbesian or Nietzschean realists who stressed an inherent lust for power and dominance.[102]

Although the classical realists successfully turned American international relations scholarship away from liberal internationalism, they soon faced challenges from neorealists who took inspiration from more positivist concepts of theory. The key text here was Kenneth N. Waltz's influential *Theory of International Politics*.[103] On the one hand, Waltz rejected the classical realists' appeals to the alleged laws of human nature – our sinfulness or lust for power. He dismissed philosophical anthropologies as unhelpful for a value-free, scientific theory. On the other hand, however, he echoed the classical realists' focus on the sovereign state in contrast to positivist concepts such as systems, transactions, and processes. He dismissed the systems theories of Stanley

---

[100] N. Guilhot (ed.), *The Invention of International Relations Theory: Realism, the Rockefeller Foundation, and the 1954 Conference on Theory* (New York: Columbia University Press, 2011).

[101] K. Deutsch, *The Nerves of Government: Models of Political Communication and Control* (London: Free Press of Glencoe, 1963); John W. Burton, *International Relations: A General Theory* (Cambridge: Cambridge University Press, 1965).

[102] See, especially, A. Freyberg-Inan, *What Moves Man: The Realist Theory of International Relations and Its Judgment of Human Nature* (New York: SUNY Press, 2003).

[103] K. N. Waltz, *Theory of International Politics* (New York: Addison-Wesley, 1979), pp. 38–59.

Hoffmann, Kaplan, and Richard Rosecrance as offering mere taxonomies or frameworks of vaguely defined parts without clear causal relationships. Waltz sought, in other words, to forge a positivist science – a systematic theory – of the 'bounded realm or domain of activity' that was constituted by the interactions of states.[104]

Waltz's picture of international relations was simple. If we assume the basic units of international relations are sovereign states, and if we grant that sovereign states acknowledge no superior authority, then we can agree that states exist in a condition of anarchy. Furthermore, if we recognize that states have unequal resources and capabilities, we can also agree that there is hierarchy in this anarchy. Waltz thus presented international relations theory as the explanation of the patterns that we see in international relations by reference to a structure of anarchy and hierarchy and its disciplining effects on states.[105] Waltz drew explicitly here on an analogy with economic theories of the market. He said little about the nature of the state, apart from that it was the most important unit in international relations just as the firm was in market economies. He even argued that if scholars wanted to explain foreign policies, they had to look at a wide range of variables, including constitutions, customs and habits, and individual beliefs.[106] When Scott Sagan claimed that Waltz assumed states were rational actors, Waltz replied emphatically that he did not.[107] Waltz treated states as unitary actors but not necessarily as rational ones.

Nonetheless, Waltz's followers did begin to explain the behaviour of states by reference to, in older realist terms, the pursuit of interests or, in newer economic terms, the maximization of utility. Neorealism thus became tied not to the statecraft of Morgenthau and his peers but, rather, to a more positivist theory. This rational choice theory came from economics and it differed significantly from sociology theories of functions and systems. For a start, rational choice theory tried to base itself on axioms, stated in a formal language, and then deductively to derive conclusions from those axioms. In addition, the axioms of rational choice were generally associated with explicit micro-level assumptions about the rationality of individuals or at times of states. Within the study of international relations, rational choice, game theory, and bargaining theory initially flourished in studies of foreign policymaking, interstate bargaining, and interstate cooperation. Later, precisely because the policy agendas of

---

[104] Ibid., p. 8. [105] Ibid., p. 69.

[106] K. Waltz, *Foreign Policy and Domestic Politics* (1967); and for discussion, I. Hall, 'The Second Image Traversed: Kenneth N. Waltz's Theory of Foreign Policy', *Australian Journal of Political Science*, 49 (2014), 535–41.

[107] See, especially, S. D. Sagan and K. N. Waltz, *The Spread of Nuclear Weapons: A Debate Renewed* (New York: W. W. Norton, 2003).

realism and liberalism have no intrinsic connection to particular visions of a scientific agenda, other rational choice scholars, including Robert Keohane, began to use similar theoretical ideas to explore institutions. These 'neoliberal institutionalists' might have adopted rational choice theory instead of the legalism and functionalism of earlier liberal internationalists, but they still sought to resurrect liberal institutionalism as a counterpoint to neorealism.[108]

Liberal internationalism continued to gain adherents even during the ascendency of classical realism. Plenty of liberals continued to study and promote international organizations and laws, dismissing a reduction of politics to interests and power. This liberalism, like realism, is less a vision of a scientific discipline than an account of politics combined with a policy agenda. One can again imagine historicists, modernists, positivists, and others all debating its validity. Nonetheless, just as the neorealists loosely tied their realism to rational choice theory, so from the late 1970s onwards liberals loosely associated their agenda with sociological theories of regimes, institutions, and norms. These liberals did not appeal to sociological theories and concepts as part of a positivist agenda to create a general theory. They were modernists fending off the challenge of both rational choice and realism by appealing to mid-level theories of norms and identities as alternatives to a general theory of interests and power.

In the mid-1970s, John Ruggie introduced the concept of a 'regime' to refer to the 'mutual expectations, generally agreed-to rules, regulations and plans in accordance with which organizational energies and financial commitments are allocated'.[109] Ruggie and Ernst Haas used the concept of a regime to discuss a 'collective response', partly at the international level, to technological and environmental issues. In so far as the concept of a regime was primarily descriptive, it initially could attract scholars with diverse theoretical commitments. When Stephen Krasner edited a special issue of *International Organization* on regimes, for example, he labelled Ruggie, Keohane, and implicitly himself, as 'modified' structural realists.[110] Ironically, Ruggie's own contribution to the same special issue clearly distanced himself from both realism and rational choice. Ruggie located his approach to regimes against rather than within realism, specifically contrasting his approach to that of both Krasner and Waltz.

---

[108] R. O. Keohane, *Neorealism and its Critics* (New York: Columbia University Press, 1986).

[109] J. Ruggie, 'International Responses to Technology: Concepts and Trends', *International Organization*, 29 (1975), 558, 567–9. Also see E. Haas, 'On Systems and International Regimes', *World Politics*, 27 (1975), 147–74.

[110] S. Krasner, 'Structural Causes and Regime Consequences: Regimes as Intervening Variables' in S. Krasner (ed.), *International Regimes* (Ithaca, NY: Cornell University Press, 1983), pp. 1–21.

Ruggie's main argument was that of a liberal internationalist rejecting realism. He complained that Krasner and Waltz engaged regimes only in relation to a narrow concern with power, whereas political authority was really a 'fusion of power with legitimate social purpose'.[111] Ruggie combined this complaint with that of a modernist rejecting rational choice theory. He argued that the study of regimes should focus not on power and interests but on the identities and ideas that shape how states and other actors understand their interests. Thus a regime 'involves not only the institutional grid of the state and of the international political order, through which behaviour is acted out, but also epistemes through which political relationships are visualized'.[112] Unsurprisingly, neoliberal institutionalists, such as Keohane, were unhappy with the fusion of liberal internationalism and modernism. They distinguished two approaches to 'international institutions'; their approach blended liberal internationalism with soft rational choice, Ruggie's blended liberal internationalism with what soon became known as 'social constructivism'.[113]

The English School

With the obvious exception of the neoliberal institutionalists, the American study of international relations became increasingly bifurcated between a rational choice realism and a constructivist liberalism. Once again, however, we should be wary of treating America as a paradigmatic case. Elsewhere liberal internationalism interacted more with Marxism and critical theory than with neorealism and rational choice.

In the interwar era, Britain's international policy agendas concerned Empire at least as much as internationalism. Even liberals often argued that the British Empire could promote progressive values and so secure peace.[114] The British study of international relations paid particularly close attention to imperial administration and diplomacy within a commonwealth of nations.[115] After the

---

[111] J. Ruggie, 'International Regimes, Transactions and Change: Embedded Liberalism in the Postwar Economic Order' in Krasner (ed.), *International Regimes*, p. 198.

[112] Ruggie, 'International Responses', p. 569.

[113] R. Keohane, 'International Institutions: Two Approaches', *International Studies Quarterly*, 32 (1988), 379–96.

[114] J. Morefield, *Covenants without Swords: Idealist Liberalism and the Spirit of Empire* (Princeton: Princeton University Press, 2005). For the parallels with continental liberalism and the difference made by realism, see M. Koskenniemi, *The Gentle Civilizer of Nations: The Rise and Fall of International Law, 1870–1960* (Cambridge: Cambridge University Press, 2004).

[115] Compare V. Thakur, A. Davis, and P. Vale, 'Imperial Mission, "Scientific Method": An Alternative Account of the Origins of IR', *Millennium* 46 (2017), 3–23. We should distinguish specific policy issues arising out of Empire and Commonwealth from broader conceptual ones relating to race. On the importance of the latter in American scholarship, see R. Vitalis, *White World Order, Black Power Politics* (Ithaca, NY: Cornell University Press, 2015).

Second World War, the English School of international relations scholarship continued to privilege topics that were central to British policy agendas. Broadly speaking, it echoed the classical realists' opposition to positivism while replacing their focus on power and interests with an attention to international society and diplomacy.

Herbert Butterfield spent much of the interwar years opposing the developmental nature of Whig historiography.[116] Nonetheless, he was also sceptical of social science, believing that history provided a better training for both scholars and practitioners. His rigorous 'science' or 'geometry' of 'statecraft' was, therefore, not about identifying covering laws, but about historical studies of the rules of thumb with which 'statesmen' maintained international order. Because Butterfield believed that peace was a result of politicians acting on correct beliefs, his 'science' focussed on the beliefs of eighteenth-century European diplomacy, for, he argued, the diplomacy of that age had reached a peak of sophistication, dedicating itself to maintaining a balance of power by keeping ideology and moralism out of international society. Butterfield pressed these views at the early meetings of the British Committee on the Theory of International Politics. In the Preface to one of the English School's founding texts, he and Martin Wight argued:

> That statecraft is an historical deposit of practical wisdom growing very slowly; that the political, diplomatic, legal and military writers who might loosely be termed 'classical' have not been superseded as a result of recent developments in sociology or psychology, and that it is a useful enterprise to explore the corpus of diplomatic and military experience in order to reformulate its lessons in relation to contemporary needs.[117]

The whole text echoed the classical realists' rejection of positivism for a kind of natural law while tying that law to diplomacy rather than to sin or a lust for power.

Although Butterfield and Wight referred to 'international society', this concept acquired a slightly different meaning in the other founding text of the English School. Hedley Bull's *The Anarchical Society* was written in Australia but taken to heart in Britain following its author's appointment to the Montague Burton Chair in International Relations at Oxford in the year the book was published.[118] Although Bull gestured towards historical and philosophical

---

[116] M. Bentley, *The Life and Thought of Herbert Butterfield: History, Science and God* (Cambridge: Cambridge University Press, 2011).

[117] H. Butterfield and M. Wight, 'Preface' in H. Butterfield and M. Wight (eds.), *Diplomatic Investigations: Essays on the Theory of International Politics* (London: Allen & Unwin, 1966), pp. 12–3.

[118] H. Bull, *The Anarchical Society: A Study of Order in World Politics* (London: Macmillan, 1977).

concerns, his approach was more markedly indebted to modernism. In particular, Bull analysed international society less as a historical achievement than as an institution made up of constituent parts and obeying basic rules. Again, although Bull often used the word 'institution', he took it and its meaning from the functionalism of modernist anthropology. Indeed, Bull, like Wight, expressed distain for 'formal' institutions such as the United Nations. He focussed instead on social institutions conceived as the bundles of norms and practices that sustained civilized international conduct in a society of states – international law, diplomacy, and even, in some circumstances, war. Although Bull drew on modernism, he nonetheless echoed both classical realists and Butterfield when he identified himself with a 'classical approach' defined in contrast to a 'scientific approach' within which he included positivist quantification, Kaplan's systems theory, and early examples of rational choice and game theory.[119]

The English School developed a liberal internationalism focussed on diplomatic relations and moral norms among a society of states. Unsurprisingly, they therefore provided readymade allies for Ruggie and the social constructivists in their battles with neorealists and rational choice theory. Equally, however, there were important differences between these groupings. British scholars of international relations increasingly defined themselves in contrast to their American counterparts not only methodologically but also politically. Many of them opposed not only rational choice but also American foreign policy. When Bull contrasted his classical approach with a scientific approach, he noted, without endorsing, the extent to which British observers objected to the political uses of American scholarship, particularly in nuclear strategy and the conduct of limited wars.

Throughout the 1970s and 1980s, British scholars were more interested in Marxism, critical theory, and normative agendas, all of which typically opposed American policy, than they were in theoretical debates with rational choice theorists. For a start, the 'inter-paradigm debate' pitted the English School against Marxists. The Marxists rejected ideas of international society in favour of analyses of capitalism as a 'world system'.[120] And they rejected a focus on relations between states for one on global class relations, power, and inequality. Development studies and international political economy in particular took on a distinctly Marxist hue within British universities and some nongovernmental organizations. In addition, British scholars drew on various traditions to initiate

---

[119] H. Bull, 'International Theory: The Case for a Classical Approach', *World Politics*, 18 (1966), 361–77.

[120] On this group, see I. Hall, *Dilemmas of Decline: British Intellectuals and World Politics, 1945–75* (Berkeley: University of California Press, 2012), pp. 163–9.

a 'normative turn' in the study of international relations. Some members of the English School, especially Wight, had extended their interest in the history of diplomacy to an interest in the history of international thought. Now Andrew Linklater's *Men and Citizens in the Theory of International Relations*, which, like Bull's *Anarchical Society*, was written in Australia, blended the history of international thought and critical theory.[121] Linklater opened the British sub-field to critical approaches such as those of the American Richard Ashley, the Canadian Robert Cox, and especially the German Jürgen Habermas.[122] These critical theorists and their British followers challenged the structure of international relations from the perspective of the marginal, poor, and oppressed. Finally, the impact of Marxism, and especially critical theory effectively, split the legacy of the English School itself. A dwindling group of conservatives or 'pluralists' continued to promote an order of sovereign states connected by diplomacy within an international society. A larger group of 'solidarists' wanted to use critical theory to interrogate and transform international society. The latter generally saw American constructivism as just another 'problem-solving' approach that lightly revised older realisms and institutionalisms without addressing the fundamental problems of power and inequality.[123] British scholars therefore often define themselves, in contrast to their American counterparts, as engaged with more qualitative and critical approaches, including feminism and post-colonialism.

Within the subfield of international relations, policy agendas have often played a larger role than abstract theories about the discipline of political science. Events outside the discipline have therefore often been major drivers of intellectual change. The liberal internationalism that dominated the interwar years was primarily a response to the First World War. Fascism and the Second World War inspired the rise of both a more pessimistic realism and alternative internationalisms, including a renewed interest in functional agencies. Although disciplinary historians sometimes project realism back as far as ancient Greece, the twentieth-century debate between realists and liberals was a response to these events. American scholarship has generally continued to revolve around realist and liberal policy agendas at least as much as methodological or theoretical claims about the nature of social science. British scholarship was shaped by different policy agendas built on the commonwealth and diplomacy. Its liberal

---

[121] Linklater taught at the University of Tasmania from 1976 to 1981 and then at Monash University until 1992, when he returned to the United Kingdom to a Chair at Keele University.

[122] See especially A. Linklater, *Beyond Realism and Marxism: Critical Theory and International Relations* (Houndmills: Macmillan, 1990).

[123] S. Smith, 'Paradigm Dominance in International Relations: The Development of International Relations as a Social Science', *Millennium: Journal of International Studies*, 16 (1987), 197.

internationalism privileged a society of states and norms. Its rivals came not from a realist agenda built around national interests but from a Marxist agenda built around power and inequality.

5 Neoliberalism and After

When political scientists write their own history, they tend to describe trends and debates within the discipline and, at times, to locate these within their social and political contexts. They appeal to social and political changes to explain intellectual trends in the disciple. Think, for example, of the way I earlier appealed to fascism and the Second World War to make sense of trends in international relations. Political scientists are far less likely to appeal to intellectual trends in political science to make sense of changes in society and politics. If you are not a social scientist, you might find that surprising. Surely, it is obvious that whenever policymakers adopt a policy that presupposes a method or a theory devised by social scientists, social science plays a role in creating the policy. When policymakers introduce Keynesian policies, for example, surely Keynes' ideas and their reception have to be part of any explanation of that policy.[124] Yet, there are systematic reasons why political scientists often neglect the role of their discipline in creating the world. As we have seen, modernism privileges formal explanations that either treat ideas as variables or simply ignore ideas entirely.

Although some political scientists allow for the way social science creates the world, the majority neglect it and they do so for systematic reasons. If we take seriously the ways in which social science creates the world, we cast doubt on the way the majority of political scientists understand their ideas and their discipline.[125] Imagine that rational choice theorists created a formal model that perfectly fitted some empirical phenomena, say, for example, the behaviour of legislators in the US Congress. Rational choice theorists would be likely to say that the empirical phenomena were evidence of the validity of the model and indeed of rational choice theory. In contrast, if we allow for the creative role of the social sciences, we have to allow that the model might fit only because the relevant actors have adopted the kind of self-interested posture that rational choice theory ascribes to them. That is to say, we have to allow that the model and rational choice theory might not be straightforwardly correct but rather a kind of self-fulfilling prophecy. In this section, I discuss the history of political science since the 1970s, paying particular attention to its relationship to

---

[124] P. Hall, (ed.), *The Political Power of Economic Ideas: Keynesianism across Nations* (Princeton: Princeton University Press, 1989).

[125] Compare J. Blakely, *We Built Reality: How Social Science Infiltrated Culture, Politics, and Power* (Oxford: Oxford University Press, 2020).

changing policy agendas. My point is that political scientists do not just describe and explain the world; they also make it.

Modernism and the State

Modernism transformed the concept of the state and encouraged its expansion. When modernists rejected historical narratives, they challenged the concept of the state as arising out of a nation bound by a common language, culture, and past. Furthermore, when modernists turned from a focus on the state to topics such as political parties and interest groups, they studied these sub-state institutions in terms of cross-cultural synchronic regularities rather than a shared culture or history. They thus increasingly portrayed the state as fragmented into factional interests associated with different classes and parties. In doing so, they threatened the idea that representative democracy was a way of electing and holding to account politicians who would act in accord with the common good of a pre-political nation. Representative democracy could seem, therefore, to be in danger of losing much of its legitimacy.

However, modernism also opened up new ways of making and legitimating public policy in representative democracies. Crucially, modernism inspired a new belief in formal expertise. Public policy could thus seem legitimate if it were based on the formal knowledge of modernist social science itself. Elected representatives no longer needed to express a national character and common good. They could define policy goals and check the activity of experts. Social scientists, professionals, and generalist civil servants could use their expertise to devise rational scientific policies in accord with these goals. Modernist social science thus helped to create the conditions for the administrative state. States became far more hands-on in their conduct of economic policy and in taking responsibility for their citizens' welfare. New governmental departments focussed on education, health, industry, and social welfare proved greedy for technocratic knowledge from the modernist social sciences.

We have already met the two leading forms of modernist expertise that fed into the administrative state. Although both of them stand in contrast to developmental historicism, they instantiate different formal concepts of rationality tied to different forms of explanation.[126] On the one hand, the economic concept of rationality privileges utility maximization; it arose with neoclassical theory and spread to rational choice. On the other hand, the sociological concept of rationality privileges appropriateness in relation to social norms; it arose with functionalism and spread to network theory and communitarianism.

---

[126] B. Barry, *Sociologists, Economists, and Democracy* (London: Macmillan, 1970).

Neoclassical economics instantiates a modernist concept of rationality that emphasizes atomization, deduction, and synchronic analysis. Economic rationality is a property of individual decisions and actions; it is not tied to norms, practices, or societies apart from when these are being judged as effective or ineffective ways of aggregating individual choices. In addition, economic rationality is postulated as an axiom on the basis of which to construct deductive models; it is not deployed as a principle by which to interpret facts discovered through inductive empirical research. Finally, the models derived from the axioms of economic rationality are applied to general patterns irrespective of time and space; they do not trace the particular evolution of individuals, practices, or societies. Although modernism set the scene for the economic concept of rationality, the concept took its specific content from utility maximization. In neoclassical economics, individuals act in order to maximize their personal utility, where utility is defined as a measure of the satisfaction gained from a commodity or other outcome.

The most prominent alternatives to the economic concept of rationality are a cluster of sociological ones, all of which replace instrumentality with appropriateness. Sociological rationality is about acting in accord with appropriate social norms to fulfil established roles in systems, processes, institutions, or practices. Some sociologists, including Emile Durkheim and Pierre Bourdieu, argue that even modern individuals are best conceived not as instrumental actors but as followers of social norms and roles. Others, including Max Weber and Herbert Marcuse, express fears about the spread of selfish, acquisitive, and instrumental norms in modern societies. These two strands of modernist sociology can come together in broad condemnations of modernity, capitalism, or consumerism for spreading selfish and instrumental norms that wreck older forms of solidarity and community.

In the post-war era, political science had a symbiotic relationship with the state. Political science provided the state with expertise, and the state funded political science through the rapid expansion of public universities and generous research grants. Unsurprisingly, large parts of political science developed institutions and agendas that reflected the state's priorities. In America, for example, the Vietnam War led the federal government to increase research funding on comparative politics, developing states, and rural insurgencies. Universities responded by expanding their political science departments and creating research units based on area studies. Comparative politics became probably the most prestigious and certainly the largest of the discipline's subfields. Scholars generated numerous accounts of modernization, often tying them at least loosely to systems theory and functionalism.[127]

---

[127] For a longer historical perspective, see Gilman, *Mandarins of the Future*; and M. Latham, *Modernization as Ideology: American Social Science and 'Nation Building' in the Kennedy Era* (Chapel Hill: University of North Carolina Press, 2000).

Political science's relationship to the state changed during the 1970s with the rise of neoliberalism. The state tried to roll back its research funding and soon introduced novel assessment exercises to direct its spending on higher education. The state also began to look to different types of knowledge, drawing more from business schools, promoting hi-tech, and even within the social sciences, privileging American politics and public policy over comparative politics and international relations, and privileging economic approaches over sociological theories. Unsurprisingly, political science departments have adapted to these new priorities, cutting back on faculty in comparative politics, and especially area studies, and promoting the fields now favoured by the state. It would be a mistake, however, to see the changes solely in terms of the state's impact on social science. Social scientists provided political actors with the theories they used both to narrate the crisis of the state and to develop neoliberal and other policy agendas.

Large parts of the history of political science in the late twentieth century consist of modernism turning on itself. This history also appears in the theories and reforms with which people conceived of the crisis of the state and responded to it. Although these theories and reforms challenged the expertise embedded in the post-war state, they did not challenge the more general idea of applying modernist expertise to social life. Rather, political scientists and policy actors turned to alternative forms of modernist expertise. Analytically, we can distinguish once again two forms of expertise, each of which inspired a wave of public sector reforms. The first wave of reforms echoed the economic concept of rationality; neoliberalism promoted the new public management and contracting-out. The second wave echoed the sociological concept of rationality; the third way promoted joined-up governance, networks, and partnerships.

Neoliberalism

Oversimplifications will abound in any attempt to differentiate the plethora of ideas that fed into narratives about the crisis of the state in the late twentieth century. Nonetheless, one way of approaching these narratives is as products of the two leading forms of modernist expertise. Some narratives of the crisis of the state challenged bureaucracy, corporatism, and social welfare by drawing on the economic concept of rationality. Neoclassical micro-level assumptions informed, for example, narratives that tried to show fiscal crises were a pathology built into the welfare state. These narratives went as follows.[128] Citizens, being rational actors, try to maximize their short-term interests,

---

[128] See, for example, A. King, 'Overload: Problems of Governing in the 1970s', *Political Studies*, 23 (1975), 284–96.

privileging welfare policies that are of benefit to them as individuals over the long-term, cumulative, and shared effects of rising state expenditure. Similarly, politicians, being rational actors, try to maximize their short-term electoral interests, promoting policies that will gain the votes of these rational citizens rather than pursuing fiscal responsibility. Narrow political considerations thereby trump economic imperatives. Groups of voters demand more and more welfare benefits, and politicians constantly pass welfare legislation on behalf of these voters. A growing proportion of the national product goes on welfare, making fiscal crises inevitable. These narratives of state overload and state crisis pointed to a clear solution – fiscal austerity, monetary control, and a rolling back of the state.

I will use the term 'neoliberal' broadly to refer to these economic narratives and the reforms they inspired.[129] Neoliberals compared the state's top-down, hierarchical organization with the decentralized, competitive structure of the market. They argued that the market was superior. They concluded that when possible markets or quasi-markets should replace bureaucracy. A quest for efficiency led them to call on the state to transfer organizations and activities to the private sector. Organizations could be transferred by privatization, that is, the transfer of state assets to the private sector through flotations or management buyouts. Activities could be transferred by means of contracting out, that is, the state could pay a private sector organization to undertake tasks on its behalf.

Neoliberalism drew heavily on strands of neoclassical economics such as monetarism. In addition, however, it drew on broad approaches to social science, notably rational choice theory, which themselves drew inspiration from neoclassical economics. Rational choice theory first developed during the 1950s and 1960s, but with the exception of William Riker and the department he led at Rochester, it had little impact on political science.[130] It was only as the sociological theories of the behavioural era lost favour that rational choice theory arose to offer both an appealing account of why they had failed and a proposed way forward. On the one hand, because rational choice drew on the modernist vision of theory, it could inherit the mantle of 'science' from the

---

[129] P. Mirowski and D. Plehwe (eds.), *The Road from Mont Pelerin: The Making of the Neoliberal Thought Collective* (Cambridge, MA: Harvard University Press, 2009); N. Olsen, *The Sovereign Consumer: A New Intellectual History of Neoliberalism* (Basingstoke: Palgrave Macmillan, 2019); D. Stedman Jones, *Masters of the Universe: Hayek, Friedman, and the Birth of Neoliberal Politics* (Princeton: Princeton University Press, 2014).

[130] On the earlier history of rational choice theory, see S. Amadae, *Rationalizing Capitalist Democracy: The Cold War Origins of Rational Choice Liberalism* (Chicago: University of Chicago Press, 2003). On Riker in relation to theoretical agenda of Easton and other behaviouralists, see E. Hauptmann, 'Defining "Theory" in Postwar Political Science' in G. Steinmetz (ed.), *The Politics of Method in the Human Sciences: Positivism and its Epistemological Others* (Chapel Hill, N.C.: Duke University Press, 2005), pp. 207–32.

behaviouralists. But, on the other hand, because it drew on economic rather than sociological modernism, it could escape the sense of theoretical failure that had come to surround behaviouralism and instead promote a new road to scientific knowledge.

Rational choice deployed the economic concept of rationality in ways that set it apart from other approaches to political science. For a start, rational choice relied on explicit micro-level assumptions about individuals. Rational choice theorists complained that the macro-level claims of earlier sociological theories were divorced from an account of individual choices and their unintended collective consequences. In addition, rational choice turned these micro-level assumptions into positive axioms, often stated in a formal language, from which it could use the techniques of deductive logic to prove conclusions. Although some sociological theorists had extolled deductive reasoning, they had not made their arguments 'positive' or 'formal' in the sense that rational choice theorists gave to these terms, so rational choice theorists could criticize sociological reasoning as loose and indeterminate. Some scholars of American politics adopted rational choice, with its rigorous deductive logic and formal modelling techniques, as early as the 1960s. However, the use of formal models only really took off in the mid- and late 1970s. Rational choice theorists then used the concept of a structure-induced equilibrium to include institutional arrangements in models.[131] And they further expanded their repertoire by drawing on the new economics of organizations developed by economists such as Oliver Williamson.[132] By the mid-1980s articles using formal techniques made up about a fifth of the *American Political Science Review*.[133]

Neoliberal states relied on rational choice as well as economic theories. One clear example is the public sector reforms associated with the new public management. Neoliberals believed that the discipline of the market validated the management practices of the private sector. They redefined public officials as managers or service providers, and they redefined citizens as consumers or service users. In doing so, neoliberals drew on rational choice analyses of principal–agent theory. Neoclassical economists first developed principal–agent theory to analyse the problem of delegated discretion in the private sector.[134] They argued that delegating decision-making from principals

---

[131] K. Shepsle, 'Institutional Arrangements and Equilibrium in Multidimensional Voting Models', *American Journal of Political Science*, 23 (1979), 27–60; K. Shepsle and B. Weingast, 'Structure-Induced Equilibria and Legislative Choice', *Public Choice*, 37 (1981), 503–19.

[132] T. Moe, 'The New Economics of Organization', *American Journal of Political Science*, 28 (1984), 739–77.

[133] Sigelman, 'Coevolution', 469.

[134] J. Stiglitz, 'Principal and Agent' in *The New Palgrave: A Dictionary of Economics*, 3 (1987), 966–71.

(shareholders) to agents (managers) is risky because the agents may act on their own interests. Economists proposed minimizing this risk by using incentives and market mechanisms to align the interests of the agents with those of the principals. In the public sector, the principals are the voters and their elected representatives, while the agents are public officials. For rational choice theorists, therefore, just as the basic problem of private sector corporations was to ensure managers acted on behalf of the shareholders, so the basic problem of public administration was to ensure public officials work on behalf of citizens. Neoliberals extended to the public sector the incentives and market mechanisms that economists had devised to bring the interests of agents into alignment with those of their principals. The result was the new public management.[135]

Many political scientists are sceptical that ideas play a causal role in public policy. They might object that the previous paragraph points to similarities between ideas and reforms without providing any evidence that the ideas helped to produce the reforms. It is worth saying, therefore, that my claim is not that particular politicians read academic articles, reflect on them, and draw inspiration from them. My claim is that social science feeds into the work of think tanks, policy advisers, and even high journalism, thereby becoming part of a climate of opinion that sets a policy agenda. We have clear evidence of this process.

New Zealand was arguably the first state to adopt the new public management, and its reforms certainly inspired other states. The New Zealand reforms arose from a small group of politicians, advisers, civil servants, and lobbyists associated with the Labour government of 1984–90. A Treasury document of 1987 clearly outlined their theoretical grounding in the ideas I have just discussed.[136] Ralph Chapman was one of the Treasury civil servants who developed the reform agenda. He trained as an economist before doing a PhD at the University of Auckland, in which he used formal models to analyse renting and buying as housing choices. Chapman wrote about the reforms, rightly emphasizing that their debt to principal–agent theory set them apart from the more generic managerialism associated with similar reforms in states such as the United Kingdom.[137] Later, when the New Zealand government

---

[135] M. Barzelay, *The New Public Management* (Berkeley: University of California Press, 2001); and C. Pollitt and G. Bouckaert, *Public Management Reform: A Comparative Analysis* (Oxford: Oxford University Press, 2000).

[136] Treasury, *Government Management: Briefing to the Incoming Government 1987*, vol. 1 (Wellington: Treasury, 1987). For general discussion see J. Boston, J. Martin, J. Pallot, and P. Walsh, *Public Management: The New Zealand Model* (Auckland: Oxford University Press, 1996); on the role of policy elites, see S. Goldfinch, 'Remaking New Zealand's Economic Policy: Institutional Elites as Radical Innovators, 1984–1993', *Governance*, 11 (1998), 177–207.

[137] R. Chapman, 'To Rent or Buy? Housing Tenure Choice in New Zealand', PhD Thesis, University of Auckland, New Zealand (1981); R. Chapman, 'Core Public Sector Reform in New Zealand and the United Kingdom', *Public Money & Management*, 9 (1989), 44–9.

commissioned a report on the reforms, it turned to Allen Schick. Schick was an American Professor of Public Policy who studied public budgeting because he was interested in applying the axioms of rational choice to collective decisions and because he believed 'budgeting was society's way of solving' the problem of ranking alternatives.[138] His generally favourable report echoed Chapman in its distinction between the contractualism of the reforms and a more generic managerialism.

New Institutionalisms

While some narratives of the crisis of the state embedded the economic concept of rationality, others drew on a sociological modernism. These narratives implied that the state had to change in response to international and domestic pressures. The international pressures arose because the increased mobility of capital made it more difficult for states to direct economic activity. The state could not go it alone but, rather, had to pursue coordination and regulation across borders. Industries that had operated in the domain of the state had become transnational in their activities. The growing role of transnational corporations raised problems of coordination and questions of jurisdiction. There was a gap between the national operation of regulatory structures and an increasingly international economy. The domestic pressures arose because the state confronted rising demands from citizens unhappy with both its hand-ling of the economy and its unresponsiveness. Many states were saddled with large debts. Globalization provoked anxieties about competitiveness and wages. Sections of the public worried that the state had lost control. Equally, state actors often found that they were subject to varied and even contradictory demands from the public. Voters wanted better services and lower taxes. They wanted a more effective state but also a more transparent and accountable one. They wanted decisive leaders and yet more popular participation.

I will use the term 'third way' broadly to refer to reforms inspired by these sociological narratives of the crisis of the state.[139] The third way bought into aspects of the neoliberal critique of hierarchical organization, but it had at most a circumscribed faith in the market, seeing markets as socially embedded institutions that depended on the states and societies within which they operate.

---

[138] A. Schick, *The Spirit of Reform: Managing the New Zealand State Sector in a Time of Change* (Wellington: State Services Commission, 1996). For his background, see C. Sateriale, 'Interview with Professor Allen Schick', *Public Financial Management Blog* (21 September 2011), retrieved January 9, 2022, from *https://blog-pfm.imf.org/pfmblog/2011/09/interview-with-professor-allen-schick-.html*. For discussion, see J. Wallis, 'The Schick Report: Evaluating State Sector Reform in New Zealand', *Agenda*, 4 (1997), 489–94.

[139] For discussion, see M. Bevir, *New Labour: A Critique* (London: Routledge, 2005); and A. Finlayson, 'Third Way Theory', *Political Quarterly*, 70 (1999), 271–9.

The third way suggested that in most circumstances networks offered a better source of efficiency and effectiveness. This view encouraged states not only to promote networks and partnerships but also to bring organizations together in joined-up or whole-of-government approaches to policy problems.

The third way drew heavily on social science theories, notably the new institutionalism, that arose as sociological responses to the challenge of first positivism and then rational choice. These theories are some of the most confused and confusing within political science. This confusion is a result of their highly ambiguous relationship to human agency and historical explanation. On the one hand, they try to fend off positivism and rational choice by defending the importance of agency, history, and context. On the other hand, they remain trapped within a modernism that pushes them to reject agency, history, and context in favour of formal explanations that at least gesture towards reified norms and institutions. Because the new institutionalists and their ilk are unaware of their own historical inheritance, they cannot resolve the ambiguities and confusions that beset their concepts and theories.

Some modernist empiricists responded to positivism by redefining their approach in terms of a comparative, historical, and sociological study of states. The state thus became the foci for a diverse range of substantive agendas, including comparative political economy, the political development of America, and the study of revolutions.[140] This agenda appears most importantly in the Committee on States and Social Structures set up by the Social Science Research Council in the early 1980s with Peter Evans and Theda Skocpol as chairs and Albert Hirschman, Peter Katzenstein, Ira Katznelson, Stephen Krasner, Dietrich Rueschemeyer, and Charles Tilly as its members. These political scientists complained, first, that behaviouralist attempts to replace the concept of the state with that of 'the political system' had resulted in a reductionism that neglected the potential autonomy of the state. Paradoxically, they thus tied modernist empiricism to neostatism when in fact it had arisen as political scientists tried to get behind constitutional pieties to examine actual behaviour and processes. They complained, second, that behaviouralist attempts to deduce universally valid hypotheses from general theories

---

[140] See P. Evans, D. Rueschemeyer, and T. Skocpol (eds.), *Bringing the State Back In* (New York: Cambridge University Press, 1985); and on how neostatism allegedly entailed a return to history, I. Katznelson, 'The State to the Rescue? Political Science and History Reconnect', *Social Research*, 59 (1994), 719–37. For examples of the substantive agendas, see, respectively, P. Evans, *Dependent Development: The Alliance of Multinational, State, and Local Capital in Brazil* (Princeton: Princeton University Press, 1979); S. Skowronek, *Building a New American State: The Expansion of National Administrative Capacities, 1877–1920* (Cambridge: Cambridge University Press, 1982); and T. Skocpol, *States and Social Revolutions: A Comparative Analysis of France, Russia, and China* (Cambridge: Cambridge University Press, 1978).

resulted in a lack of sensitivity to different social and historical contexts. Paradoxically, they thus associated modernist empiricism with a resistance to ahistorical claims when in fact it had arisen as social scientists introduced atomization, analysis, correlation, and classification as alternatives to the narratives of the developmental historicists.

Modernist empiricists redefined their approach yet again at the close of the twentieth century in response to the rise of rational choice theory. Rational choice theory replicated many of the features of behaviouralism that had challenged modernist empiricism; it too offered an abstract general theory from which to deduce other theories or hypotheses that could be applied and tested empirically. However, rational choice theory replaced the behaviouralists' focus on systems with one on micro-level foundations. It thus posed forcefully the question: what micro-theory could make sense of neostatism – and modernist empiricism more generally – with its dependence on analytic induction, variables, classifications, and correlations?

Neostatists and other modernist empiricists responded to the challenge of rational choice theory by rearticulating their approach as a 'new institutionalism'. However, because Riker and others already were calling for a new analysis of institutions based on rational choice theory itself,[141] modernist empiricists quickly began distinguishing their 'sociological' or 'historical' institutionalism from a 'rational choice' one.[142] Here modernist empiricists defined their new institutionalism using many of the buzzwords with which they had earlier described neostatism. They described it as a comparative and historical approach to the construction of mid-range theories out of case studies and small-N studies. Once again, however, this self-characterization makes sense only in contrast to a universal and deductive approach now associated with rational choice theory. It obscures the new institutionalists' continuing commitment to atomization and analysis – and even dependent and independent variables – as methods of generating correlations and typologies.[143] The new institutionalists' rejection of historicism appears in their characteristic

---

[141] W. Riker, 'Implications from the Disequilibrium of Majority Rule for the Study of Institutions', *American Political Science Review*, 74 (1980), 432–47.

[142] See, for example, P. Hall and R. Taylor, 'Political Science and the Three Institutionalisms', *Political Studies*, 44 (1996), 936–57; and K. Thelen and S. Steinmo, 'Historical Institutionalism in Comparative Politics' in S. Steinmo, K. Thelen, and F. Longstreth (eds.), *Structuring Politics: Historical Institutionalism in Comparative Analysis* (New York: Cambridge University Press, 1992), pp. 1–32.

[143] The persistent need to fend off universal, deductive theory surely explains why some new institutionalists want to assimilate rational-choice theory to structural functionalism, as when Skocpol calls the structural functionalists 'forebears' of rational choice theory, and rational choice theorists the 'successors' of the Grand Theorists of old. See T. Skocpol, 'Theory Tackles History', *Social Science History*, 24 (2000), 675–6.

difficulties when addressing the very micro-level issues that rational choice theory poses so forcefully. Sometimes they simply wish these issues away by pronouncing them unhelpful obstacles to our tackling big substantive problems. At other times, they unpack their approach in terms of the micro-theory of rational choice, thereby undermining the very distinctions they had been so concerned to draw.[144] They almost never analyse institutions in terms of a micro-theory of contingent and competing beliefs and actions, for, if they did so, they would undermine the possibility of treating institutions as stable objects that can be known through correlations and classifications.

When modernist empiricists inspired by sociological theories of rationality studied neoliberal reforms of the public sector, they were often highly critical. They argued that the reforms exasperated problems of coordination and steering, and they promoted networks and joined-up government as solutions to these problems.[145] Advocates of networks distinguish them from hierarchies as well as markets. Old institutionalists believed that hierarchies made it easier to tackle many social problems by dividing them into smaller tasks, each of which could then be performed by a specialized unit. New institutionalists argue that this hierarchic approach to problem-solving no longer suits today's world. They claim that policymakers confront 'wicked problems' that are not amenable to division and specialization; these problems require networks not hierarchies.

The concept of a 'wicked problem' arose as part of an amorphous modernist empiricism associated with the new institutionalism, organization theory, and functionalism.[146] Social democrats often adopted it to counter neoliberalism. Wicked problems are usually defined in terms such as the following: a problem of more or less unique nature; the lack of any definitive formulation of such a problem; the existence of multiple explanations for it; the absence of a test to decide the value of any response to it; all responses to it being better or worse rather than true or false; and each response to it having important consequences such that there is no real chance to learn by trial and error. Typically these features strongly imply that wicked problems are interrelated. For example, a particular wicked problem might be explained in terms of its relationship to others, or any response to it might impact others. Classic examples of wicked

---

[144] For these two approaches to micro-theory, see, respectively, P. Pierson and T. Skocpol, 'Historical Institutionalism in Contemporary Political Science' in I. Katznelson and H. Milner (eds.), *Political Science: The State of the Discipline* (New York: W.W. Norton, 2002), pp. 695–6; and P. Pierson, 'Increasing Returns, Path Dependence, and the Study of Politics', *American Political Science Review*, 92 (2000), 251–67.

[145] See, for example, R. Rhodes, *Understanding Governance* (Buckingham: Open University Press, 1997).

[146] H. Rittel and M. Webber, 'Dilemmas in a General Theory of Planning', *Policy Sciences*, 4 (1973), 155–69.

problems include pressing issues of governance such as security, the environment, and urban blight.

New institutionalists usually accept neoliberal arguments about the inflexible and unresponsive nature of hierarchies, but instead of promoting markets, they appeal to networks as a suitably flexible and responsive alternative based on recognition that social actors operate in structured relationships. They argue that efficiency and effectiveness derive from stable relationships characterized by trust, social participation, and voluntary associations. In their view, while hierarchies can provide a context for trust and stability, the time for hierarchies has passed. Hierarchies do not suit the new knowledge-driven global economy. This new world increasingly throws up wicked problems that require networks and joined-up governance. A new institutionalism, with its sociological concept of rationality, thus inspired a second wave of reforms, including Australia's whole-of-government agenda, New Labour's 'Third Way', post-9/11 security policy in the United States, and international attempts to deal with failed states.[147]

After Neoliberalism

We have seen that in the late twentieth century, political science inspired two waves of public sector reform. One promoted market technologies derived from neoclassical economics. The other promoted the different technologies of networks, partnership, and inclusion, all derived from sociological theories of institutions and systems. Contemporary governance characteristically relies on a mixture of technologies. It is all too easy to postulate a monolithic neoliberalism characterized by market technologies, the individualization of the self, or the erosion of the public sphere. In practice, however, the contemporary state is messy, lacking any such centre. It draws on diverse market, institutionalist, and other technologies. I do not want to imply that these technologies work as advertised. On the contrary, as public servants and citizens draw on local traditions that bare little relation to academic social science, so they act in ways that intentionally or unintentionally transform and thwart these technologies.

Although these technologies rarely work, they continue to influence public policy. Here we might identify at least three other technologies that now coexist with the markets and networks already discussed. Each illustrates the way in which policy technologies arise out of interdisciplinary spaces where political science draws on theories from other social sciences.

Evidence-based approaches spread from health sciences and healthcare. Typically, they rely on either large data sets or more usually randomized control

---

[147] M. Bevir, *Democratic Governance* (Princeton: Princeton University Press, 2010).

trials to establish that some treatment or drug has a high probability of success even if there is no particular causal theory explaining why it does so. Since the 2010s, these approaches have spread to all sorts of policy fields. Policymakers identify interventions, anticipate outcomes, and specify ways of measuring those outcomes. They randomly assign the policy intervention to target groups while also monitoring designated control groups. They are thus able to compare the changes in the target group with a control group that did not experience the intervention. Advocates describe the approach as 'test, learn, adapt'.[148]

Nudge technologies arose out of behavioural economics. This behavioural economics tries to correct for the simplicities of the economic concept of rationality by drawing on psychological accounts of ways in which people are characteristically irrational. It seeks to modify economics by, for example, allowing that people characteristically put more emphasis on the short term and less on the long term than they should if they were strictly rational in economic terms. Nudge theorists suggest that governments should use people's heuristics and other irrationalities to steer them towards the choices the government wants them to make.[149] Governments might, for example, create short-term incentives to nudge people to make long-term investments in their private old age pensions.

Finally, the concept of resilience arises out of engineering and ecology. Engineers have long accepted that buildings and systems are subject to errors and shocks that can lead them to fail. Resilience is the ability of a building or system to absorb errors and shocks without totally failing. Engineers often design and maintain infrastructure in ways that promote such resilience. Ecologists extended the concept of resilience from these physical systems to biological ones. Ecosystems should be resilient or self-reliant in that they can adapt and survive. Other social scientists further extended the concept to both local communities and individuals. Resilient communities are able to use their own assets, rather than government assistance, to respond to disasters and generally to improve their own social and economic conditions. Resilient individuals are, similarly, those who have the resources to recover from physical, mental, or economic adversity. In recent years, government and voluntary organizations have adopted policies seeking to build resilience among vulnerable communities and people.[150]

---

[148] L. Haynes, O. Service, B. Goldacre, and D. Torgerson, *Test, Learn, Adapt: Developing Public Policy with Randomised Controlled Trials* (London: Cabinet Office, 2012).

[149] P. Dolan, M. Hallsworth, D. Halpern, D. King, and I. Vlaev, *Mindspace: Influencing Behaviour through Public Policy* (London: Cabinet Office, 2010).

[150] Risk and Regulation Advisory Council, *Building Resilient Communities, from Ideas to Sustainable Action* (London: RRAC, 2009).

6 The Revenge of History

Clearly, this Element portrays political science from an alternative perspective to those that dominate the discipline. I have rejected modernist forms of explanation that privilege formal classifications, correlations, and models over history. I have instead told a historical story that emphasizes the contestability and contingency of the emergence of political science as part of a wider modernism, the conjoining of positivist theory with behavioural topics and quantitative techniques, and the relationship of political science to the state.

Throughout I have emphasized the messiness of history in contrast to internal disciplinary histories that suggest some kind of intellectual progress in a realm of pure inquiry. The history of political science is less one of scholars testing and improving theories by reference to data than of their appropriating and transforming ideas, often obscuring or obliterating their former meanings, to serve new purposes in shifting rhetorical and political contexts.[151] Section 2 suggested that the discipline does not study a given and shared empirical domain; rather, it was made as modernists turned from historicism to atomized facts and formal explanations. Section 3 implied that its assumptions do not necessarily go together; rather, behaviouralism yoked together a disjointed set of empirical topics, statistical methodologies, and grand theories. Section 4 suggested that it is not monolithic; rather, different subfields draw on different histories and assumptions to construct the objects they study in different ways. Section 5 implied that it does not offer neutral accounts of an external world; rather, it influences actions and policies in ways that help create the very world it purports to analyse.

Political science contains warring factions that promote diverse ideas but forget the history of those ideas even as they forge them anew in the heat of a different battle. What is the history of my own perspective? Does it too have a place in political science? To answer these questions, we need to look at the Cinderella of the discipline's subfields – political theory.

Political Theory

The success of behaviouralism redefined the relationship of political theory to the rest of the discipline. Political science became increasingly separate from political theory, with its focus on the history of western political thought. Political scientists sought new 'positive' theories with little reference to the history of political thought or normative theory. Although political theorists could not ignore behaviouralism, they could come out swinging against it.

---

[151] F. Nietzsche, *On the Genealogy of Morality*, K. Ansell-Pearson (ed.), C. Diethe (trans.) (Cambridge: Cambridge University Press, 2007), p. 51.

Leo Strauss was among the first to offer a new vision of theory.[152] He attacked both historicism and positivism, revitalized the study of canonical texts, and seemingly promoted a conservative vision of natural right. Although left-leaning theorists rejected his politics, they too defended the canon and opposed behaviouralism. In Berkeley, in the late 1960s, Sheldon Wolin argued that political theorists had a different 'vocation' from the rest of the discipline.[153] Political theory had been the nearest thing to a common core in the discipline. Now it was the locus of hostility – whether conservative, radical, or some confused blend of them – to the discipline's scientific pretensions.

Since the 1960s, innovations in political theory have often had interdisciplinary roots in either philosophy or history. Some of these innovations seemed to rebuild political theory on modernist principles. For a start, some historians of political thought argued that to understand a text one had to place it in its particular historical context. In their view, canonical texts address historical debates, not perennial problems that remain relevant to us. Some historians, including Quentin Skinner, echoed modernism in arguing that we have to adopt a proper method in order to secure facts against which then to evaluate rival theories and interpretations.[154] In addition, some analytic philosophers, including John Rawls, developed ideal theories that seemed to stand apart from both historical and empirical studies.[155] Political philosophy could thus seem to be a type of applied ethics. In this view, political philosophy discusses the ends we should adopt and political science discusses how best to realize these ends.

Other innovations in political theory were more clearly opposed to modernist political science. Although we should be wary of imposing commonalities on the relevant theorists, most were historicists. Typically, they reasserted historicism but without the developmentalism that was so widespread in the nineteenth century. Their historicism inspired a shared scepticism towards typologies, correlations, and models, suggesting that modernist social science did not attend sufficiently to history. To be more specific, their historicism suggested that typologies, correlations, and models are objectifications that hide the historicity of both the objects they depict and the modes by which they do so. Equally, their historicism rejected developmental narratives with their principles of reason,

---

[152] L. Strauss, *Natural Right and History* (Chicago: University of Chicago Press, 1953).

[153] S. Wolin, *Politics and Vision* (Princeton: Princeton University Press, 1960).

[154] J. Tully (ed.), *Meaning and Context: Quentin Skinner and his Critics* (Cambridge: Polity Press, 1988).

[155] J. Rawls, *A Theory of Justice* (Cambridge, MA: Belknap Press, 1971); K. Forrester, *In the Shadow of Justice: Postwar Liberalism and the Remaking of Political Philosophy* (Princeton: Princeton University Press, 2019); A. Galisanka, *John Rawls: The Path to A Theory of Justice* (Cambridge, MA; Harvard University Press, 2019).

character, and progress, turning instead to a novel stress on dispersal, difference, and discontinuity.

This reassertion of historicism occurred in both the history of political thought and political philosophy. Among historians of political thought, Skinner himself seems to have stopped associating himself with his earlier modernist claims about methods and facts. Recently, he has even begun to describe his histories as genealogies.[156] Most political theorists influenced by Skinner show little interest in his earlier methodological claims. They just write narratives that focus on ideas in contexts and thereby at least implicitly challenging appeals to more formal causes. Arguably the main source of inspiration for historical genealogies is, however, Michel Foucault. Foucault's own early work suggests a debt not only to French histories of reason but also structuralism; he can seem to rely on the formalism and rejection of agency that characterize structuralism and modernism more generally.[157] As he turned to genealogies, however, he clearly renounced appeals to underlying structures or systems – the internal relations among the units that allegedly defined a practice or language.[158] He concentrated instead on multiple surfaces in constant states of emergence, displacement, conquest, and flux. Where his earlier works had presented a series of discrete synchronic moments, his genealogies introduced history as diachronic movement.

Some political philosophers also reasserted historicism. The two most important examples – Alasdair MacIntyre and Charles Taylor – had been involved in the British New Left and its conscious attempt to reread Marx to stress his debt to Hegel. Both MacIntyre and Taylor wrote scathing critiques of positivist political science and its concept of causation, its neglect of intentionality, and its atomism.[159] They also challenged the ideal theory that became prominent in analytic political philosophy, promoting a more historicist approach to ethics by drawing on Hegel, hermeneutics,

---

[156] Q. Skinner, 'A Genealogy of the Modern State', *Proceedings of the British Academy*, 162 (2009), 325–370; J. Prinz and P. Raekstad, 'The Value of Genealogies for Political Philosophy', *Inquiry* (forthcoming).

[157] H. Dreyfus and P. Rabinow, *Michel Foucault: Beyond Structuralism and Hermeneutics* (Chicago: University of Chicago Press, 1983); G. Gutting, *Michel Foucault's Archaeology of Scientific Reason* (Cambridge: Cambridge University Press, 1989).

[158] M. Foucault, 'Nietzsche, Genealogy, History' in P. Rabinow (ed.), *The Foucault Reader* (New York: Pantheon Books, 1984), pp.76–100. C. Koopman, *Genealogy as Critique: Foucault and the Problems of Modernity* (Stanford: Stanford University Press, 2013).

[159] A. MacIntyre, 'A Mistake about Causality in the Social Sciences' in P. Laslett and W. Runciman (eds.), *Philosophy, Politics, and Society* (Oxford: Basil Blackwell, 1962), pp. 48–70; C. Taylor, 'Interpretation and the Sciences of Man', *Review of Metaphysics*, 25 (1971), 3–51; J. Blakely, *Alasdair MacIntyre, Charles Taylor, and the Demise of Naturalism* (Notre Dame: University of Notre Dame Press, 2016).

and phenomenology.[160] Other philosophers, notably Peter Winch, drew on the work of Ludwig Wittgenstein to make similar arguments within the philosophy of social science.[161] Winch argued that the social sciences were not properly sciences at all; they aimed at understanding, unpacking webs of meaning, rather than at causal explanation.

Most of the political theorists discussed so far made their careers in history or philosophy departments. Nonetheless, their historicism proved congenial to theorists in political science departments looking to develop a critical perspective on the rest of the discipline. Hanna Pitkin was, for example, a colleague of Wolin's at Berkeley. She drew on Wittgenstein to offer a historicist critique of political science akin to those already discussed.[162] It should perhaps come as little surprise, therefore, to find that the political theorists who have written critical histories of political science – the forerunners of this Element, if you will – have often been Pitkin's students or students of her students: Jack Gunnell, Terry Ball, James Farr, Emily Hauptmann, and more recently, Robert Adcock.

Competing Perspectives

On offer, then, are two contrasting approaches to political science: one modernist and broadly formal, the other historicist and broadly interpretive. Modernists seek stable and formal concepts, categories, and typologies. They try to operationalize these concepts in comparisons, correlations, and models. Sometimes they, or people influenced by them, translate their findings into scientific expertise on policy issues. In contrast, historicists seek to recover the intentionality of actions. They try to understand beliefs and desires by locating them in webs of belief, intellectual traditions, and cultural contexts. Sometimes they, or people influenced by them, draw on their understanding to engage people in dialogue and discussion. In this Element, I have told the history of the former approach in theoretical terms taken from the latter.

Someone might reasonably ask: how can we decide between these two contrasting approaches? Actually, as modernism and historicism contain contrasting approaches within themselves, the more general question is, how can

---

[160] A. MacIntyre, *A Short History of Ethics* (London: Macmillan, 1966); C. Taylor, *Sources of the Self: The Making of the Modern Identity* (Cambridge, MA: Harvard University Press, 1989).

[161] P. Winch, *The Idea of a Social Science and Its Relation to Philosophy* (London: Routledge, 1958).

[162] H. Pitkin, *Wittgenstein and Justice: On the Significance of Ludwig Wittgenstein for Social and Political Thought* (Berkeley: University of California Press, 1972); T. Ball, E. Hauptmann, J. Gunnell et al., 'Symposium: The Berkeley School of Political Theory', *PS: Political Science and Politics*, 50 (2017), 789–810; and Hauptmann, 'Defining "Theory" in Postwar Political Science', pp. 207–32.

we decide among any number of approaches – behaviouralism, rational choice, institutionalism, realism, historicism, and yet others?

To conclude, I want to suggest that part of the answer to this question is that we can assess approaches to political science by reference to the history of political science. Obviously, I do not mean that the history of political science has an inherent rationality such that the allegedly best approach comes to dominate it. Instead, I mean that we can ask how capable each of these approaches is of providing a historical account of itself and its rivals. Because these approaches play a role in constructing their privileged facts and their explanatory logics, they are loosely incommensurable: any attempt to justify an approach by reference to its privileged facts and explanations looks perilously circular. The evaluation of these approaches requires us to compare them by reference to a shared subject matter. Political scientists might find just such subject matter in the history of the discipline.

Crucially, because approaches to political science are effectively approaches to human life, they present themselves at least implicitly as being capable of analysing and explaining the history of the discipline. If behaviouralism, rational choice, institutionalism, realism, and historicism are valid approaches to human action, presumably they also apply to those actions and practices that constitute political science. Each approach needs to show that it works with respect to the part of human life that is the history of political science. Furthermore, when these approaches narrate the history of the discipline, they engage one another in a way that generates something like a shared subject matter: a rational choice history of political science has to explain the rise and content of institutionalism, an institutionalist history of the discipline has to explain the rise and content of rational choice, and so on.

Some readers might think the idea of modernist histories of the discipline is faintly absurd. Certainly, if rational choice theorists narrated the history of rational choice to suggest it was a product of strategic actors promoting their own interests, they would give us little reason to think rational choice is true. Similarly, if institutionalists narrated institutionalism as a product of path dependency and critical junctures, we would surely take that as a reason to doubt the validity of the approach. What do these absurdities imply? On the one hand, they surely imply that historicism is a far more viable theory of human life and so politics than are these modernisms. On the other hand, they suggest that modernists might defend their approaches not as true theories that capture reality but, rather, as admitted simplifications that help us to generate beneficial knowledge.

Today, modernists often present their approaches as just such simplifications. Rational choice theorists defend their models as heuristics.[163] Institutionalists defend their approach as a series of 'as-if' assumptions.[164] The key questions then become what are the benefits of such simplifications given that they are admittedly false. Modernists might argue that they generate crucial policy advice by which we can solve collective problems. Critics might argue that they merely give rise to flawed attempts to control and govern us through, for example, quasi-markets and joined-up institutions.

---

[163] J. Barkin, 'On the Heuristic Use of Formal Models in International Relations Theory', *International Studies Review*, 17 (2015), 617–34.

[164] C. Hay, 'Neither Real nor Fictitious but "as if Real"? A Political Ontology of the State', *British Journal of Sociology*, 65 (2014), 459–80.

Bibliography

Adams, H. (1892). The Germanic Origins of New England Towns. *John Hopkins University Studies in Historical and Political Science*, 2, 5–38.

Adams, H. (1884). Special Methods of Historical Study. *Johns Hopkins University Studies in Historical and Political Science*, 1, 25–137.

Adams, H. (1895). Is History Past Politics? *Johns Hopkins University Studies in Historical and Political Science*, 3, 68–75.

Adcock, R. (2003). The Emergence of Political Science as a Discipline: History and the Study of Politics in America, 1875–1910. *History of Political Thought*, 24, 481–508.

Adcock, R. (2007). Interpreting Behavioralism. In R. Adcock, M. Bevir and S. Stimson, eds., *Modern Political Science: Anglo-American Exchanges since 1880*. Princeton: Princeton University Press, pp. 181–208.

Adcock, R. (2014a). A Disciplinary History of Disciplinary Histories: The Case of Political Science. In R. Backhouse and P. Fontaine, eds., *A Historiography of the Modern Social Sciences*. Cambridge: Cambridge University Press, pp. 211–36.

Adcock, R. (2014b). *Liberalism and the Emergence of American Political Science: A Transatlantic Tale*. Oxford: Oxford University Press.

Aksu, E. ed. (2008). *Early Notions of Global Governance: Selected Eighteenth-Century Proposals for 'Perpetual Peace'*. Cardiff: University of Wales Press.

Almond, G. (1960). A Functional Approach to Comparative Politics. In G. Almond and J. Coleman, eds., *The Politics of the Developing Areas*. Princeton: Princeton University Press, pp. 3–64.

Almond, G. (1965). A Developmental Approach to Political Systems. *World Politics*, 17, 183–214.

Almond, G. (1995). Political Science: The History of the Discipline. In R. Goodin and H. Klingemann, eds., *A New Handbook of Political Science*. Oxford: Oxford University Press, pp. 50–96.

Amadae, S. (2003). *Rationalizing Capitalist Democracy: The Cold War Origins of Rational Choice Liberalism*. Chicago: University of Chicago Press.

Aristotle. (1946). *The Politics*, trans. E. Barker. Oxford: Clarendon Press.

Baer, M., Jewell, M., and Sigelman, L., eds. (1991). *Political Science in America: Oral Histories of a Discipline*. Lexington: University Press of Kentucky.

Ball, T., Hauptmann, E., Gunnell, J. et al. (2017). Symposium: The Berkeley School of Political Theory. *PS: Political Science and Politics*, 50, 789–810.

Bancroft, G. (1860–74). *A History of the United States from the Discovery of the American Continent to the Present Time*, 8 vols. Boston: Little, Brown.

Barker, E. (1915). *Political Thought in England from Herbert Spencer to Present Day*. New York: Holt.

Barker, E. (1944). *The Development of Public Services in Europe, 1660–1930*. New York: Oxford University Press.

Barkin, J. (2015). On the Heuristic Use of Formal Models in International Relations Theory. *International Studies Review*, 17, 617–34.

Barry, B. (1970). *Sociologists, Economists, and Democracy*. London: Macmillan.

Barzelay, M. (2001). *The New Public Management*. Berkeley: University of California Press.

Beard, C. (1961). *An Economic Interpretation of the Constitution*. New York: Macmillan.

Beer, S. (1956). Pressure Groups and Parties in Britain. *American Political Science Review*, 50, 1–23.

Beer, S. (1958). The Analysis of Political Systems. In S. Beer and A. Ulam, eds., *Patterns of Government: The Major Political Systems of Europe*. New York: Random House, pp. 3–68.

Beer, S. (1963a). Causal Explanation and Imaginative Re-enactment. *History and Theory*, 3, 6–29.

Beer, S. (1963b). *Modern British Politics: A Study of Parties and Pressure Groups*. London: Faber.

Beer, S. (1970). Political Science and History. In M. Richter, ed., *Essays in Theory and History: An Approach to the Social Sciences*. Cambridge, MA: Harvard University Press, pp. 41–73.

Bentley, M. (2011). *The Life and Thought of Herbert Butterfield: History, Science and God*. Cambridge: Cambridge University Press.

Bevir, M. (1999). *The Logic of the History of Ideas*. Cambridge: Cambridge University Press.

Bevir, M. (2002). Sidney Webb: Utilitarianism, Positivism, and Social Democracy. *Journal of Modern History*, 74, 217–52.

Bevir, M. (2005). *New Labour: A Critique*. London: Routledge.

Bevir, M. (2010). *Democratic Governance*. Princeton: Princeton University Press.

Blakely, J. (2016). *Alasdair MacIntyre, Charles Taylor, and the Demise of Naturalism*. Notre Dame: University of Notre Dame Press.

Blakely, J. (2020). *We Built Reality: How Social Science Infiltrated Culture, Politics, and Power*. Oxford: Oxford University Press.

Blondel, J. (1981). *Discipline of Politics*. London: Butterworth.

Boston, J., Martin, J., Pallot, J., and Walsh, P. (1996). *Public Management: The New Zealand Model*. Auckland: Oxford University Press.

Bremner, G. and Conlin, J., eds. (2015). *Making History: Edward Augustus Freeman and Victorian Cultural Politics*. Oxford: Oxford University Press.

Bryce, J. (1888). *The American Commonwealth*, 3 vols. London: Macmillan.

Bryce, J. (1909). Presidential Address to the Fifth Annual Meeting of the American Political Science Association. *American Political Science Quarterly*, 3, 10–6.

Bryce, J. (1921). *Modern Democracies*, 2 vols. London: Macmillan.

Bull, H. (1966). International Theory: The Case for a Classical Approach. *World Politics*, 18, 361–77.

Bull, H. (1977). *The Anarchical Society: A Study of Order in World Politics*. London: Macmillan.

Burgess, J. (1891). *Political Science and Comparative Constitutional Law*, 2 vols. Boston: Ginn.

Burgess, J. (1897). Political Science and History. In *Annual Report of the American Historical Association for the Year 1896*. Washington, DC: Government Printing Office, pp. 201–20.

Burgess, J. (1934). *Reminiscences of an American Scholar*. New York: Columbia University Press.

Burrow, J. (1966). *Evolution and Society*. Cambridge: Cambridge University Press.

Burrow, J. (1981). *A Liberal Descent: Victorian Historians and the English Past*. Cambridge: Cambridge University Press.

Burton, J. (1965). *International Relations: A General Theory*. Cambridge: Cambridge University Press.

Butler, D., and Stokes, D. (1969). *Political Change in Britain: Forces Shaping Electoral Choice*. New York: St. Martin's Press.

Butterfield, H., and Wight, M. (1966). Preface. In H. Butterfield and M. Wight, eds., *Diplomatic Investigations: Essays on the Theory of International Politics*. London: Allen & Unwin, pp. 11–3.

Campbell, A., Miller, W., and Converse, P. (1960). *The American Voter*. Chicago: University of Chicago Press.

Chapman, R. (1981). To Rent or Buy? Housing Tenure Choice in New Zealand. Ph.D. Thesis, New Zealand: University of Auckland.

Chapman, R. (1989). Core Public Sector Reform in New Zealand and the United Kingdom. *Public Money & Management*, 9, 44–9.

Collini, S. (1988). 'Disciplinary History' and 'Intellectual History': Reflections on the Historiography of the Social Sciences in Britain and France. *Revue de Synthese*, 3, 387–99.

Collini, S. (1991). *Public Moralists: Political Thought and Intellectual Life in Britain 1850–1930*. Oxford: Oxford University Press.

Collini, S. (2009). Postscript: Disciplines, Canons, and Publics: The History of 'The History of Political Thought' in Comparative Perspective. In D. Castiglione and I. Hampsher-Monk, eds., *The History of Political Thought in National Context*, Cambridge: Cambridge University Press, pp. 280–302.

Collini, S., Winch, D., and Burrow, J. (1983). *That Noble Science of Politics*. Cambridge: Cambridge University Press.

Crowther-Heyck, H. (2005). *Herbert A. Simon: The Bounds of Reason in Modern America*. Baltimore: Johns Hopkins University Press.

den Otter, S. (1996). *British Idealism and Social Explanation*. Oxford: Clarendon Press.

Deutsch, K. (1963). *The Nerves of Government: Models of Political Communication and Control*. London: Free Press of Glencoe.

Dickinson, G. (1926). *The International Anarchy, 1904–1914*. New York: The Century.

Dolan, P., Hallsworth, M., Halpern, D., King, D., and Vlaev, I. (2010). *Mindspace: Influencing Behaviour through Public Policy*. London: Cabinet Office.

Dreyfus, H., and Rabinow, P. (1983). *Michel Foucault: Beyond Structuralism and Hermeneutics*. Chicago: University of Chicago Press.

Easton, D. (1953). *The Political System: An Inquiry into the State of Political Science*. New York: Knopf.

Easton, D., Gunnell, J., and Graziano, L. (1991). *The Development of Political Science: A Comparative Survey*, New York: Routledge.

Englander, D., and O'Day, R., eds. (1995). *Retrieved Riches: Social Investigation in Britain, 1880–1914*. Aldershot: Scolar Press.

Evans, P. (1979). *Dependent Development: The Alliance of Multinational, State, and Local Capital in Brazil*. Princeton: Princeton University Press.

Evans, P., Rueschemeyer, D., and Skocpol, T., eds. (1985). *Bringing the State Back In*. New York: Cambridge University Press.

Everdell, W. (1997). *The First Moderns*. Chicago: University of Chicago Press.

Farr, J. (1988). Political Science and the Enlightenment of Enthusiasm. *American Political Science Review*, 82, 51–69.

Farr, J. (1991). Political Science and the State. In J. Brown and D. van Keuren, eds., *The Estate of Social Knowledge*. Baltimore: Johns Hopkins University Press, pp. 1–21.

Farr, J. (1995). Remembering the Revolution. In J. Farr, J. Dryzek, and S. Leonard, eds., *Political Science in History: Research Programs and Political Traditions*. Cambridge: Cambridge University Press, pp. 198–224.

Finer, H. (1921). *Foreign Governments at Work: An Introductory Study.* New York: Oxford University Press.

Finer, H. (1970). *Theory and Practice of Modern Government.* Westport, CT: Greenwood Press.

Finlayson, A. (1999). Third Way Theory. *Political Quarterly,* 70, 271–9.

Forrester, K. (2019). *In the Shadow of Justice: Postwar Liberalism and the Remaking of Political Philosophy.* Princeton: Princeton University Press.

Fortes, M., and Evans-Pritchard, E. (1940). *African Political Systems.* London: Oxford University Press.

Foucault, M. (1984). Nietzsche, Genealogy, History. In P. Rabinow, ed., *The Foucault Reader.* New York: Pantheon Books, pp.76–100.

Frei, C. (2001). *Hans J. Morgenthau: An Intellectual Biography.* Baton Rouge: Louisiana State University Press.

Freyberg-Inan, A. (2003). *What Moves Man: The Realist Theory of International Relations and Its Judgment of Human Nature.* New York: SUNY Press.

Friedrich, C. (1929). Review of Quantitative Methods in Politics. *American Political Science Review,* 23, 1022–7.

Friedrich, C. (1937). *Constitutional Government and Politics.* New York: Harper.

Friedrich, C. (1941). *Constitutional Government and Democracy.* Boston: Little, Brown.

Friedrich, C. (1952). *The Age of the Baroque, 1610–1660.* New York: Harper.

Friedrich, C. (1953). Comments on the Seminar Report. *American Political Science Review,* 47, 658–61.

Galisanka, A. (2019). *John Rawls: The Path to A Theory of Justice.* Cambridge, MA: Harvard University Press.

Gilman, N. (2003). *Mandarins of the Future: Modernization Theory in Cold War America.* Baltimore: Johns Hopkins University Press.

Goldfinch, S. (1998). Remaking New Zealand's Economic Policy: Institutional Elites as Radical Innovators, 1984–1993. *Governance,* 11, 177–207.

Goodin, R., and Klingemann, H.-D. (1998). Political Science: The Discipline. In R. Goodin and H.-D. Klingemann, eds., *A New Handbook of Political Science.* Oxford: Oxford University Press, pp. 1–49.

Griffith, E., ed. (1948). *Research in Political Science.* Chapel Hill: University of North Carolina Press.

Guilhot, N., ed. (2011). *The Invention of International Relations Theory: Realism, the Rockefeller Foundation, and the 1954 Conference on Theory.* New York: Columbia University Press.

Gunnell, J. (2007). Making Democracy Safe for the World: Political Science between the Wars. In R. Adcock, M. Bevir, and S. Stimson, eds., *Modern Political Science: Anglo-American Exchanges since 1880*. Princeton: Princeton University Press, pp. 137–57.

Gutting, G. (1989). *Michel Foucault's Archaeology of Scientific Reason*. Cambridge: Cambridge University Press.

Haas, E. (1964). *Beyond the Nation-State: Functionalism and International Organization*. Stanford: Stanford University Press.

Haas, E. (1975). On Systems and International Regimes. *World Politics*, 27, 147–74.

Hall, I. (2012). *Dilemmas of Decline: British Intellectuals and World Politics, 1945–75*. Berkeley: University of California Press.

Hall, I. (2014). The Second Image Traversed: Kenneth N. Waltz's Theory of Foreign Policy. *Australian Journal of Political Science*, 49, 535–41.

Hall, P., ed. (1989). *The Political Power of Economic Ideas: Keynesianism across Nations*. Princeton: Princeton University Press.

Hall, P., and Taylor, R. (1996). Political Science and the Three Institutionalisms. *Political Studies*, 44, 936–57.

Halliday, F. (1988). Three Concepts of Internationalism. *International Affairs*, 64, 187–98.

Hauptmann, E. (2005). Defining 'Theory' in Postwar Political Science. In G. Steinmetz, ed., *The Politics of Method in the Human Sciences: Positivism and its Epistemological Others*. Chapel Hill: Duke University Press, pp. 207–32.

Hay, C. (2014). Neither Real nor Fictitious but 'as if Real'? A Political Ontology of the State. *British Journal of Sociology*, 65, 459–80.

Haynes, L., Service, O., Goldacre, B., and Torgerson, D. (2012). *Test, Learn, Adapt: Developing Public Policy with Randomised Controlled Trials*. London: Cabinet Office.

Hayward, J., Barry, B., and Brown, A., eds. (1999). *The British Study of Politics in the Twentieth Century*. Oxford: Oxford University Press.

Heaney, M. and Hansen, J. (2006). Building the Chicago School. *American Political Science Review*, 100, 589–96.

Herbst, J. (1965). *The German Historical School in American Scholarship*. Ithaca: Cornell University Press.

Herring, P. (1929). *Group Representation before Congress*. Baltimore: Johns Hopkins University Press.

Herring, P. (1953). On the Study of Government. *American Political Science Review*, 47, 961–74.

Heyck, H. (2007). Administrative Science. In M. Bevir, ed., *Modernism and the Social Sciences: Anglo-American Exchanges, c. 1918–1980*. Cambridge: Cambridge University Press, pp. 155–81.

Heyck, H. (2015). *The Age of System: The Rise and Fracture of High Modern Social Science*. Baltimore: Johns Hopkins University Press.

Ikenberry, G. (1993). The Political Origins of Bretton Woods. In M. Bordo, J. Barry and B. Eichengreen, eds., *A Retrospective on the Bretton Woods System*. Chicago: University of Chicago Press, pp. 155–82.

Isaac, J. (2012). *Working Knowledge: Making the Human Sciences from Parsons to Kuhn*. Cambridge, MA: Harvard University Press.

Kant, I. (1949). *The Philosophy of Kant*, trans. C. Friedrich. New York: Modern Library.

Katznelson, I. (1994). The State to the Rescue? Political Science and History Reconnect. *Social Research*, 59, 719–37.

Keohane, R. (1986). *Neorealism and its Critics*. New York: Columbia University Press.

Keohane, R. (1988). International Institutions: Two Approaches. *International Studies Quarterly*, 32, 379–96.

Key, V. (1958). The State of the Discipline. *American Political Science Review*, 52, 961–71.

King, A. (1975). Overload: Problems of Governing in the 1970s. *Political Studies*, 23, 284–96.

Kloppenberg, J. (1986). *Uncertain Victory: Social Democracy and Progressivism in European and American Thought, 1870–1920*. New York: Oxford University Press.

Koopman, C. (2013). *Genealogy as Critique: Foucault and the Problems of Modernity*. Stanford: Stanford University Press.

Koskenniemi, M. (2004). *The Gentle Civilizer of Nations: The Rise and Fall of International Law, 1870–1960*. Cambridge: Cambridge University Press.

Krasner, S. (1983). Structural Causes and Regime Consequences: Regimes as Intervening Variables. In S. Krasner, ed., *International Regimes*. Ithaca: Cornell University Press, pp. 1–21.

Latham, M. (2000). *Modernization as Ideology: American Social Science and 'Nation Building' in the Kennedy Era*. Chapel Hill: University of North Carolina Press.

Lazarsfeld, P., Berelson, B., and Gaudet, H. (1944). *The People's Choice: How the Voter Makes up his Mind in a Presidential Election*. New York: Duell, Sloan, and Pearce.

Lecky, W. (1892). *The Political Value of History*. London: E. Arnold.

Linklater, A. (1990). *Beyond Realism and Marxism: Critical Theory and International Relations*. Houndmills: Macmillan.

Lippincott, B. (1940). The Bias of American Political Science. *Journal of Politics*, 2, 125–39.

Lippmann, W. (1922). *Public Opinion*. New York: Harcourt, Brace.

Lloyd, W. (1949). The United Nations and World Federalism. *The Antioch Review*, 9, 16–28.

Lowell, A. (1896). *Governments and Parties in Continental Europe*, 2 vols. Boston: Houghton, Mifflin.

Lowell, A. (1908). *The Government of England*, 2 vols. New York: Macmillan.

Lowell, A. (1913). *Public Opinion and Popular Government*. New York: Longmans.

Lowenberg, G. (2006). The Influence of European Émigré Scholars on Comparative Politics, 1925–65. *American Political Science Review*, 100, 597–604.

MacIntyre, A. (1962). A Mistake about Causality in the Social Sciences. In P. Laslett and W. Runciman, eds., *Philosophy, Politics, and Society*. Oxford: Basil Blackwell, pp. 48–70.

MacIntyre, A. (1966). *A Short History of Ethics*. London: Macmillan.

Maine, H. (1871). *Village Communities in the East and West*. London: John Murray.

Maine, H. (1917). *Ancient Law*. New York: Dutton.

Mandler, P. (2000). 'Race' and 'Nation' in Mid-Victorian Thought. In S. Collini, R. Whatmore, and B. Young, eds., *History, Religion, and Culture: British Intellectual History 1750–1950*. Cambridge: Cambridge University Press, pp. 224–44.

Mannheim, K. (1940). *Man and Society in an Age of Reconstruction: Studies in Modern Social Structure*, trans. E. Shils. London: Routledge & Kegan Paul.

McBriar, A. (1987). *An Edwardian Mixed Doubles: The Bosanquets versus the Webbs*. Oxford: Oxford University Press.

McCallum, R., and Readman, A. (1947). *The British General Election of 1945*. London: Oxford University Press.

McKay, D. (1999). *Federalism and the European Union: A Political Economy Perspective*. Oxford: Oxford University Press.

Merriam, C. (1970). The Present State of the Study of Politics. In *New Aspects of Politics*. Chicago: University of Chicago Press, pp. 63–83.

Mill, J. S. (1965). *Principles of Political Economy, Books I–II*. Vol. II of *The Collected Works of John Stuart Mill*. Toronto: University of Toronto Press.

Mirowski, P., and Plehwe, D., eds. (2009). *The Road from Mont Pelerin: The Making of the Neoliberal Thought Collective*. Cambridge, MA: Harvard University Press.

Mitrany, D. (1943). *A Working Peace System*. London: Royal Institute for International Affairs.

Mitrany, D. (1975). *The Functional Theory of Politics*. London: M. Robertson.

Moe, T. (1984). The New Economics of Organization. *American Journal of Political Science*, 28, 739–77.

Morefield, J. (2005). *Covenants without Swords: Idealist Liberalism and the Spirit of Empire*. Princeton: Princeton University Press.

Morgenthau, H. (1954). *Politics Among Nations: The Struggle for Power and Peace*. New York: Knopf.

Murphy, C. (1994). *International Organization and Industrial Change: Global Governance since 1850*. Cambridge: Blackwell.

Nietzsche, F. (2007). *On the Genealogy of Morality*, ed. K. Ansell-Pearson, trans. C. Diethe. Cambridge: Cambridge University Press.

Odegard, P. (1928). *Pressure Politics: The Story of the Anti-Saloon League*. New York: Columbia University Press.

Olsen, N. (2019). *The Sovereign Consumer: A New Intellectual History of Neoliberalism*. Basingstoke: Palgrave Macmillan.

Paul, H. (2008). A Collapse of Trust: Reconceptualizing the Crisis of Historicism. *Journal of the Philosophy of History*, 2, 63–82.

Pederson, S., and Mandler, P., eds. (1994). *After the Victorians: Private Conscience and Public Duty in Modern Britain*. London: Routledge.

Pemberton, J.-A. (2020). *The Story of International Relations*, 3 vols. London: Palgrave Macmillan.

Pierson, P. (2000). Increasing Returns, Path Dependence, and the Study of Politics. *American Political Science Review*, 92, 251–67.

Pierson, P. and Skocpol, T. (2002). Historical Institutionalism in Contemporary Political Science. In I. Katznelson and H. Milner, eds., *Political Science: The State of the Discipline*. New York: W.W. Norton, pp. 693–721.

Pitkin, H. (1972). *Wittgenstein and Justice: On the Significance of Ludwig Wittgenstein for Social and Political Thought*. Berkeley: University of California Press.

Pollitt, C., and Bouckaert, G. (2000). *Public Management Reform: A Comparative Analysis*. Oxford: Oxford University Press.

Prinz, J., and Raekstad, P. Forthcoming. The Value of Genealogies for Political Philosophy. *Inquiry*.

Radcliffe-Brown, A. (1924). The Mother's Brother in South Africa. *South African Journal of Science*, 21, 542–55.

Rawls, J. (1971). *A Theory of Justice*. Cambridge, MA: Belknap Press.

Rhodes, R. (1997). *Understanding Governance*. Buckingham: Open University Press.

Riker, W. (1980). Implications from the Disequilibrium of Majority Rule for the Study of Institutions. *American Political Science Review*, 74, 432–47.

Riker, W. (1982). The Two-Party System and Duverger's Law: An Essay on the History of Political Science. *American Political Science Review*, 76, 753–66.

Risk and Regulation Advisory Council. (2009). *Building Resilient Communities, from Ideas to Sustainable Action*. London: RRAC.

Rittel, H., and Webber, M. (1973). Dilemmas in a General Theory of Planning. *Policy Sciences*, 4, 155–69.

Rodgers, D. (1998). *Atlantic Crossings: Progressive Politics in a Social Age*. Cambridge, MA: Harvard University Press.

Rose, R. (1965). *Politics in England: An Interpretation*. London: Faber.

Ross, D. (1990). On the Misunderstanding of Ranke and the Origins of the Historical Profession in America. In G. Iggers and J. Powell, eds., *Leopold von Ranke and the Shaping of the Historical Discipline*. Syracuse: Syracuse University Press, pp. 154–69.

Ross, D. (1991). *The Origins of American Social Science*, Cambridge: Cambridge University Press.

Ross, D., ed. (1994). *Modernist Impulses in the Human Sciences, 1870–1930*. Baltimore: Johns Hopkins University Press.

Rothermund, D. (2006). Constitution Making and Decolonization. *Diogenes*, 53, 9–17.

Ruggie, J. (1975). International Responses to Technology: Concepts and Trends. *International Organization*, 29, 557–83.

Ruggie, J. (1983). International Regimes, Transactions and Change: Embedded Liberalism in the Postwar Economic Order. In S. Krasner, ed., *International Regimes*. Ithaca: Cornell University Press, pp. 195–232.

Sagan, S. and Waltz, K. (2003). *The Spread of Nuclear Weapons: A Debate Renewed*. New York: W. W. Norton.

Sateriale, C. (2011, September 1). Interview with Professor Allen Schick. *Public Financial Management Blog*. Retrieved January 9, 2022, from https://blog-pfm.imf.org/pfmblog/2011/09/interview-with-professor-allen-schick-.html

Schattschneider, E. (1935). *Politics, Pressures, and the Tariff*. New York: Prentice-Hall.

Schick, A. (1996). *The Spirit of Reform: Managing the New Zealand State Sector in a Time of Change*. Wellington State Services Commission.

Scott, W. (1992). *Chester I. Barnard and the Guardians of the Managerial State*. Lawrence: University Press of Kansas.

Seeley, J. (1896). *Introduction to Political Science*. London: Macmillan.

Shepsle, K. (1979). Institutional Arrangements and Equilibrium in Multidimensional Voting Models. *American Journal of Political Science*, 23, 27–60.

Shepsle, K., and Weingast, B. (1981). Structure-Induced Equilibria and Legislative Choice. *Public Choice*, 37, 503–19.

Sigelman, L. (2006). The Coevolution of American Political Science and the American Political Science Review. *American Political Science Review*, 100, 463–78.

Skinner, Q. (2009). A Genealogy of the Modern State. *Proceedings of the British Academy*, 162, 325–70.

Skocpol, T. (1978). *States and Social Revolutions: A Comparative Analysis of France, Russia, and China*. Cambridge: Cambridge University Press.

Skocpol, T. (2000). Theory Tackles History. *Social Science History*, 24, 669–76.

Skowronek, S. (1982). *Building a New American State: The Expansion of National Administrative Capacities, 1877–1920*. Cambridge: Cambridge University Press.

Smith, S. (1987). Paradigm Dominance in International Relations: The Development of International Relations as a Social Science. *Millennium: Journal of International Studies*, 16, 189–206.

Somit, A., and Tanenhaus, J. (1967). *The Development of Political Science: From Burgess to Behavioralism*. Boston: Allyn and Bacon.

SSRC Committee on Political Behavior. (1950). Committee Briefs: Political Behavior. *Social Science Research Council Items*, 4, 20.

Stapleton, J. (1994). *Englishness and the Study of Politics: The Social and Political Thought of Ernest Barker*. Cambridge: Cambridge University Press.

Stapleton, J. (2000). Political Thought and National Identity, 1850–1950. In S. Collini, R. Whatmore, and B. Young, eds., *History, Religion, and Culture: British Intellectual History 1750–1950*, Cambridge: Cambridge University Press, pp. 245–69.

Stedman Jones, D. (2014). *Masters of the Universe: Hayek, Friedman, and the Birth of Neoliberal Politics*. Princeton: Princeton University Press.

Stiglitz, J. (1987). Principal and Agent. *The New Palgrave: A Dictionary of Economics*, 3, 966–71.

Strauss, L. (1953). *Natural Right and History*. Chicago: University of Chicago Press.

Stubbs, W. (1904). *The Letters of William Stubbs*, ed., W. Hutton. London: Archibald Constable.

Taylor, C. (1971). Interpretation and the Sciences of Man. *Review of Metaphysics*, 25, 3–51.

Taylor, C. (1989). *Sources of the Self: The Making of the Modern Identity*. Cambridge, MA: Harvard University Press.

Thakur, V., Davis, A., and Vale, P. (2017). Imperial Mission, 'Scientific Method': An Alternative Account of the Origins of IR. *Millennium*, 46, 3–23

Thelen, K. and Steinmo, S. (1992). Historical Institutionalism in Comparative Politics. In S. Steinmo, K. Thelen, and F. Longstreth, eds., *Structuring Politics: Historical Institutionalism in Comparative Analysis*. New York: Cambridge University Press, pp. 1–32.

Treasury. (1987). *Government Management: Briefing to the Incoming Government 1987*, vol. 1. Wellington: Treasury.

Tully, J., ed. (1988). *Meaning and Context: Quentin Skinner and his Critics*. Cambridge: Polity Press.

UNESCO. (1950). *Contemporary Political Science: A Survey of Methods, Research and Teaching*. Paris: UNESCO.

Vitalis, R. (2015). *White World Order, Black Power Politics*. Ithaca: Cornell University Press.

Wallas, G. (1908). *Human Nature in Politics*. London: Archibald Constable.

Wallas, G. (1914). *The Great Society*. London: Macmillan.

Wallis, J. (1997). The Schick Report: Evaluating State Sector Reform in New Zealand. *Agenda*, 4, 489–94.

Waltz, K. (1967). *Foreign Policy and Domestic Politics*. New York: Little, Brown.

Waltz, K. (1979). *Theory of International Politics*. New York: Addison-Wesley.

Williams, A. (2007). *Failed Imagination? The Anglo-American New World Order from Wilson to Bush*. Manchester: Manchester University Press.

Winch, P. (1958). *The Idea of a Social Science and its Relation to Philosophy*. London: Routledge.

Wolin, S. (1960). *Politics and Vision*. Princeton: Princeton University Press.

Wright, Q. (1942). *A Study of War*. Chicago: University of Chicago Press.

Zimmern, A. (1936). *The League of Nations and the Rule of Law, 1918–1935*. London: Macmillan.

Acknowledgements

My research into the history of the human sciences has benefited from a series of workshops. I am grateful to everyone involved in the projects on 'Historicizing Politics', 'Historicism and the Human Sciences', and 'Modernism and the Social Sciences'. Although many of them would disagree with large parts of this Element, I learnt from them and sharpened my ideas in discussion with them. I am particularly indebted to Robert Adcock, Ian Hall, and Shannon Stimson.

Printed in the United States
by Baker & Taylor Publisher Services